ARGUMENTATION AND DEBATE

D1526987

Resolved: That the United States should significantly reform Social Security

Lawrance M. Bernabo

Communication 1600
University of Minnesota Duluth
Fall 2023

ISBN: 979-8-3908461-8-6

Preface

There are lots of debate handbooks. Dozens of them. So why not use one of those for this class?

Two reasons. The first is that the debate format we use in this class is completely different from all the types of debate for which there are existing handbooks. There is a simple reason for why we do it differently: class periods are 50 minutes long. All of the debate formats used in high school and college debate take longer than an hour (more like an hour and a half), so they just will not work in the time we have for class.

The second reason is that all of those debate handbooks are for competitive debaters, who will be debating for years, with different topics each year. They contain chapters on debate theory that go way beyond what we are doing in this class, which is introducing you to the basic principles of debate and providing practical experience by having you actually do a series of face-to-face debates with classmates.

Obviously, you are never going to do a "debate" like what we are doing in this class—where there are set speeches with proscribed time limits—in the real world. But chances are pretty good that in the real world you will be engaging in "debates," where you and others are discussing what should be done in a given situation at work, and you are coming up with reasons for and against doing something or not doing something.

Public speaking is about making a case in something of a vacuum. You pick a topic, you make your case, and that is it. But in the real world when you make a case for something, others might take an opposite position and argue against what you think should be done. In debate you learn to think about arguments from both sides, how to defend your position against attacks, and how to make a much stronger case for your position than you would if you were just giving a traditional public speech.

I would contend that learning how to develop a stronger case and being able to extend arguments in the face of opposition, are valuable skills, that will be of benefit to you in the real world after college.

Plus, they can also benefit you while you are still in college, because the skills you will be learning in this class you can also use in writing papers and answering essay questions on exams.

WHAT DO YOU NEED TO KNOW GOING INTO THIS CLASS?

There are two important things for you to know going into this class. The first is that every student who has ever taken this class has said that debate did not really make sense to them until they actually did a debate round. Doing a debate made a BIG difference.

Therefore, the goal in this class is to get you to practice rounds as quickly as possible. Fortunately, one of the legacies of the pandemic is that we have ZOOM as a resource. Before the pandemic the debates in this course involved two teams with two debaters. That meant in *two weeks* everybody in class could do *one* debate round. But with ZOOM, everybody in class can do *two* practice debates in *one week* (one on Affirmative and one on Negative).

Know that it is likely that some of the graded debate rounds will happen on ZOOM. This is dependent on how many students we end up having, because after those two practice rounds you will debate twice as the affirmative and twice as the negative and we can only do six debates a week in class. If you end up doing a ZOOM round, you will be excused from class and the two debaters will coordinate with the instructor as to when the debate will take place that day (I will be part of the ZOOM meeting, to provide feedback after the round, just like in class). Also, students who are assigned to critique the ZOOM debate (which will automatically be recorded by ZOOM), will not have to attend class that day but watch the ZOOM debate later to do their critique.

The second important thing is that this is the most front-loaded course you will ever take in your entire life. Because to do those practice rounds you must have all the evidence you need. The Affirmative is going to have several options on what they run for harms, plan planks and solvency. As Negative, you need evidence to respond to each possible option. Additionally, the Affirmative needs to have evidence to respond to all of the Plan Attacks and Disadvantages that the Negative can throw against them in a round.

So, do not be surprised when in the first three or four weeks of class you spend half of the time you will end up devoting to this class for the entire semester. Because you need to have evidence for *both* sides of *all* the voting issues before you can be cleared to do the practice rounds. That is what we focus on in the first part of the semester: Getting the evidence to be able to use in rounds to support your arguments and attacks.

Beyond that, there are several others things to be aware of with this class.

Learn from each other. You will hear more debates than you will actually debate, and from each debate you can learn a lot. Unlike public speaking, every debate is on the exact same topic you will be speaking about. This has several advantages.

For one thing, you can "steal" evidence from each other. One semester we were debating climate change and one of the harms was the increased alkaline levels in seawater. Somebody found a card arguing that the rate of increase was so insignificant, that it would take thousands of years to have an impact on human beings. That one card *destroyed* that argument, so everybody else in the class got a hold of that card to use against that harm area. Of course, everybody running that harm area stopped, because they could not win the argument against that killer card.

Remember, just because you have found enough evidence to be cleared for doing the debates, does not mean that you stop looking for evidence. There are always better cards out there, and one way of finding them is to pay attention in the rounds you are critiquing to help find even better cards.

For another thing, you will also learn to emulate what works in rounds and avoid what does not. Early on, you will see classmates drop points in a round or who fail to signpost their arguments and how doing so hurts them. This will help you learn not to do those things. But you will also see things that work, in terms of how to signpost things correctly and how to argue out voting issues specifically and explicitly, that you will want to do in your own rounds.

THE GOLD STANDARD

A couple of years ago a former student from one of my debate classes asked me to write a letter of recommendation for a scholarship awarded by the Communication Department. In my letter I explained that she had taken several courses from me and received A's in all of them.

Then I wrote that while she had the third highest grade in the debate class, that in seven of the eight debates she did during the semester (two of which were practice debates), her opponents had their *highest* grades of the semester.

The reason was quite simple. She did everything right. She signposted, she had evidence, she argued out the voting issues. She did everything a debater was supposed to do, which meant she did not create any problems for her opponents in the round by dropping a point or failing to signpost where something was supposed to be flowed.

This is why you will not be cleared to do the practice debate rounds until you have all the evidence you need. Because if you do not have the arguments and evidence cards you need going into the round, you cannot respond to the arguments and evidence of your opponent.

That student pretty much established the gold standard for what a student in *Argumentation and*

Debate should be like, and I think that is a goal to which you should aspire as well.

HAVE FUN

I think debating is fun, and I usually explain it in terms of being able to crush people with words, because debate is as competitive as any sport you can name.

Finally, keep in mind that what you learn in this class, about how to construct an argument, how to find the best possible evidence, and how to argue out your case, can benefit you in other classes. Most students do not know how to argue a case and provide appropriate evidence. Imagine how impressed your other professors will be when you do just that, whether in a paper you are writing for another class or when you "debate" points in classroom discussions.

So, have fun.

Table of Contents

Chapter 1.
Argument^1 and Argument^2

Debate is a public argument between two sides. But in the context of public debate, the term *argument* had two specific and different meanings.

Argument^1 refers to the argument that a speaker advances while Argument^2 is the argument that is being contested between the two sides.

That means in an Argument^2 between two debaters, each debater has their own Argument^1 that they are advancing, or, more accurately, a series of Argument^{1}s that support their position.

For example, if you and a friend were arguing over the merits of a movie you had just seen, that would be an Argument^2. You would justify your position in this debate that the movie was a good one with a series of Argument^{1}s in which you praised the acting, writing, cinematography, etc. Your friend would offer a different set of Argument^{1}s where they attacked the believability of the plot, the realism of the special effects, etc.

When we are talking about an Argument^1, there are three specific parts to any argument that you need to prove your point:

- Claim
- Evidence
- Warrant (Explanation of how the evidence fits the claim)

When all you have is a claim without evidence, that is <u>not</u> an argument, that is an *assertion*. In the real world an unsubstantiated claim might be effective, but in the world of argumentation—and in this class—you can refute (beat) such claims by pointing out your opponent does not have any evidence for their argument.

Does that mean that all claims *have* to have evidence? Not if they are based on common knowledge as to who is the current President of the United States, which film won the Oscar for Best Picture last year, what team is the defending World Series champion, etc. With regards to our topic of this semester, you will end up knowing more about Social Security than most Americans.

Probably more than 75%-80% of Americans. But the people who are retired and taking Social Security benefits know a lot about the system. With every debate you will learn more about Social Security and efforts to reform it, and within the context of our class and your debates there will be references in the rounds to things you all know.

Also, you can use an opponent's evidence against them, by pointing out the source is not credible, that the statistics are outdated, or that the quotation they read does not prove the claim they set up (that happens a lot: claims will overstate what the evidence actually says, so that is one of the first things you check when you hear an opponent's evidence in a round).

That being said, the goal is to have a complete argument: a clear claim with evidence that you can explain warrants that particular claim. Having evidence is not necessarily sufficient. You can claim that Donald Trump should be re-elected president, but if your evidence is that he is a billionaire, you then have to explain why that particular evidence supports (or warrants) your claim.

TYPES OF CLAIMS

There are four types of propositions that can serve as the claim in an argument:

- Proposition of Fact, e.g., "The total cost of the Social Security program for the year 2021 was $1.145 trillion." This has to be something that is not in dispute, that both sides in a debate would agree is factually true. Of course, today, lots of "facts" are held to be in dispute, but objectively something like how much money Social Security paid out in a given year should be something you should be able to prove beyond dispute.

- Proposition of Value, e.g., "Social Security provides benefits by allowing people to not just buy food and medicine, but also to help them keep their homes." This type of proposition argues that something is good or bad (i.e., to advance a specific value judgment) or that something that is in dispute (like climate change) is true or false.

- Proposition of Prediction, e.g. "If Social Security is not reformed the system will become insolvent by 2035." This type of proposition advances the likelihood of something happening—or not happening—in the future, based on current conditions and/or prospective changes.

- Proposition of Policy, e.g., "The United States should significantly reform social security." These propositions usually contain the word "should," because it advocates a change in the *status quo.*

The debate resolution is always a Proposition of Policy (what "should" be done). Your contentions and advantages will probably be Propositions of Value (e.g., a problem exists, the plan will solve it, the current system is a good one). Those contentions and advantages can be supported by claims that are Propositions of Fact and/or Value.

Because reforming Social Security is basically an economic topic, this semester there will be a lot of evidence from economists, politicians, and social scientists. Even before you begin researching the topic to find evidence, think about which of those sources would be the strongest and the weakest. If the Affirmative has evidence from an economist and the Negative has evidence from a politician, which source has more credibility? Because the qualifications of your sources is part of the calculus of who has the stronger argument.

(*Remember during the COVID pandemic when politicians dismissed the claims of scientists because the politicians said the scientists were being "political." And the politicians were not? Objectively, scientists are more credible sources than politicians. Keep that in mind when you look for sources.*)

ARGUMENT[1]S FOR AN ARGUMENT[2]

Ultimately, a debate is an Argument[2] on two levels. On the macro level the entire debate is an Argument[2], but on the micro level the debate is made up of a series of Argument[2]s. The Affirmative case argues out several points about harms and solvency. The Negative is going to try to refute those points. So there will be a series of Argument[2]s regarding harms and solvency.

Again, each side has an Argument[1] for each of those

Argument[2]s. It is important that when you come up with the claims and evidence for each Argument[1] that you are thinking of winning the Argument[2] at issue.

Chapter 2.
Social Security

If you are going to spend a semester debating Social Security, then there is some basic information about the subject that you need to know.

"Social Security" is the term commonly used for the federal Old-Age, Survivors, and Disability Insurance (OASDI) program. It is administered by the Social Security Administration (SSA). Most of the information about Social Security in this chapter comes directly from the SSA.

The original Social Security Act was enacted in 1935, and the current version of the Act, as amended by Congress, encompasses several social welfare and social insurance programs.

The average monthly Social Security benefit in November 2022 was $1,551.

The total cost of the Social Security program for the year 2021 was $1.145 trillion, which is about 5 percent of the United States Gross Domestic Product (GDP).

Although most people say they will retire between 65 and 67, most retire early (at 61) because of job loss, poor health, or caregiving responsibilities. Only

5% of men and 7% of women wait until age 70 to take Social Security benefits (delaying gets you an annual increase of 8% in benefits for each year you wait to retire). Those people who retire early have to consider spending taxable money from retirement accounts and/or converting to tax-free Roth accounts to help bridge the gap between retirement and reaching the higher retirement age. It would also reduce taxes in later years.

Social Security is funded primarily through payroll taxes under both the Federal Insurance Contributions (FICA) and the Self-Employed Contributions Act (SECA). Wage and salary earnings in covered employment, up to an amount specifically determined by law, are subject to the Social Security payroll tax. Wage and salary earnings above this amount are not taxed. In 2022, the maximum amount of taxable earnings is $147,000.

The legislation that established the OASDI tax requires that it must automatically be withheld from employee paychecks at a rate of 6.2%, making the total tax 12.4% when matched by the employer. In comparison, the Medicare tax is only 1.45%. The OASDI tax is applied to both traditional employees and self-employed individuals. If you are self-employed, this means that you are expected to pay the entire 12.4% tax on your earned income. However, self-employed workers are also permitted to deduct half of the OASDI tax paid on their annual tax filings.

Social Security is nearly universal, with 94 percent of individuals in paid employment in the United States working in covered employment. However, about 6.6 million state and local government workers in the United States, or 28 percent of all state and local workers, are not covered by Social Security but rather by pension plans operated at either the state or local level.

With few exceptions, all legal residents working in the United States now have an individual Social Security number.

Social Security payroll taxes are collected by the Internal Revenue Service (IRS) and are formally entrusted to the Federal Old-Age and Survivors Insurance (OASI) Trust Fund and the Federal Disability Insurance (DI) Trust Fund, as well as the two Social Security Trust Funds.

Social Security revenues exceeded expenditures between 1983 and 2009, which increased trust fund balances. The retirement of the large baby-boom generation, however, will lower balances. Without legislative changes, trust fund reserves are projected to be depleted in the years 2034 and 2065 for the OASI and DI funds, respectively.

Should depletion occur, incoming payroll tax and other revenue would only be sufficient to pay 76 percent of OASI benefits starting in 2035 and 92 percent of DI benefits starting in 2065.

Is Social Security going broke?

For over a half-century people have been saying that Social Security is doomed to fail. Yet for over 90 years it has been paying out benefits every month. As long as workers and employers pay payroll taxes, Social Security will not run out of money. It is a pay-as-you-go system. For decades, the program collected more than it paid out, building a surplus that stood at $2.83 trillion at the end of 2022. But the system has now started to pay out more than it takes in, mainly because not only is the retiree population growing faster than the working population, retirees are living longer.

According to Statista in 2023, in 1860 the life expectancy (from birth) in the United States was only 39.41 years, which had dropped to 35.1 by the end of the Civil War in 1865. In 1900 it was 48.19. When Social Security was established in 1935 it was 60.7. In 1965 it was 70.11, in 2000 it was 76.47 and as of 2020 life expectancy is 78.81 (which is actually a decrease from the high of 78.94 in 2015). That means Americans are living 18 years longer now than they did when Social Security began, which works out to 216 additional monthly payments for every American who is paid benefits when they retire.

Concerns are certainly warranted, because there are plenty of scare stories in the media or on the Internet about the impending doom for Social Security. The sources of these stories range from online crackpots who insist Social Security is a socialist, "deep-state" plot, and want the program to be abolished on principle, to official sources who are triggered by the annual report from the Social Security Board of Trustees, which invariably notes that the nation's social insurance program is one year closer to insolvency.

The key claim is that if no changes are made to the Social Security Program by 2035, the system would be unable to pay full benefits. However, it should be noted it was only a year ago that the prediction was insolvency by the year 2034, so we are not dealing with absolutes here (i.e., the points are debatable).

NOTE: What does "insolvency" mean in this case? That retirees no longer would receive Social Security benefits? No, it means that the program would only be bringing in enough to pay 80 percent of scheduled benefits. So the system would not collapse (pay out zero benefits), but benefits would be cut. Would that mean everybody takes a 20% cut in benefits or would different people get different amounts? Nobody knows, because there is no plan in place.

More importantly, the report says the system faces insolvency "if no changes are made to the program by 2035."

Therefore, the simple solution is that Congress implements Social Security reforms long before we get to 2035.

At this point, since you live in the real world, you are probably thinking that there is no way the Senate, controlled by the Democrats, and the House of Representative, controlled by the Republicans, will agree on *anything*, let along on Social Security.

For over a decade, Sen. Daniel Patrick Moynihan (D-New York), warned that the Social Security system was going to become insolvent if reforms were not undertaken. Every time he would say there needed to be "change," Republicans would say he wanted to "cut" social security.

After Moynihan died in 2003, there were Republican senators, part of the Tea Party Movement, who were concerned with the government's wasteful spending of money, and who warned that Social Security needed to be reformed or else it would collapse. At that point Democrats warned Republicans wanted to "cut" Social Security.

The intransience of the two political parties does not matter in the world of debate because the Affirmative has *fiat* power, which means that for the sake of debate their plan is implemented. So the Negative cannot argue that Congress will never adopt the Affirmative plan or that the President would veto it, because the Affirmative has a magic wand for the purposes of debating the resolution.

Oh, by the way, as I was researching this section, I found a piece from March of 2023 that reported the Congressional Budget Office warns that the Social Security Trust Fund will run out of money by 2033 Two years earlier than expected.

Is the Social Security retirement age 65?

Full retirement age (FRA), the age when a worker qualifies to file for 100-percent of the benefit calculated from lifetime earnings history, is 66 and 4 months for people born in 1956 and 66 and 6 months for those born in 1957. Over the next few years it will increase by two months at a time, settling at 67 for those born in 1960 and after.

When Social Security was created in 1935, 65 was set as the age of eligibility (which means you had to live five years *beyond* the life expectancy age at that point to ever get benefits, so most Americans back then would never live long enough to get benefits). In later decades, the minimum eligibility age was lowered to 62, as the age at which people could claim a reduced benefit, but 65 remained the standard for full retirement.

The 1983 overhaul of Social Security raised the retirement age to reduce Social Security's costs. The increase is being phased in over time, with 2002 being the last year in which the people being born could claim their full benefit when they turned 65. So, at what age can you retired with full benefits?

Is the annual COLA guaranteed?

Since 1975, Social Security law has mandated that benefit amounts be adjusted annually to keep pace with inflation. However, there is no requirement that the cost-of-living-adjustment (COLA) be increased each year.

The COLA is tied to a federal index of prices for select consumer goods and services called the CPI-W. Benefits are adjusted annually based on changes in the CPI-W from the third quarter of one year to the third quarter of the next. In 2022, the index showed an 8.7 percent increase in prices, so benefits will be 8.7 percent higher in 2023. That increase—caused directly by high inflation—is boosting the average retirees' monthly payments by an estimated $146.

But if the index does not show a statistically measurable rise in prices—which would happen if there is effectively no inflation that year—then there's no adjustment to benefits. This has happened three times since the current formula was adopted, in 2010, 2011 and 2016. Whether or not it produces a benefit increase, this process is automatic; it does not involve the president or

Congress. They would have to take separate action to change the COLA.

Is Social Security a Pyramid or Ponzi Scheme?

A "pyramid scheme" is a business model that recruits members with a promise of payments (or services) for enrolling others in the scheme. As recruiting multiplies, recruiting becomes quickly impossible, and most members are unable to profit, which is why they are unsustainable.

William G. Shipman of the Cato Institute argues:

> In common usage a trust fund is an estate of money and securities held in trust for its beneficiaries. The Social Security Trust Fund is quite different. It is an accounting of the difference between tax and benefit flows. When taxes exceed benefits, the federal government lends itself the excess in return for an interest-paying bond, an IOU that it issues to itself. The government then spends its new funds on unrelated projects such as bridge repairs, defense, or food stamps. The funds are not invested for the benefit of present or future retirees.[1]

---

[1] William G. Shipman, "Cato Institute Social Security Choice Paper No. 2: Retiring with Dignity: Social Security vs. Private Markets," *Cato Project on Social Security Choice*, August 14, 1995. Retrieved 2005-12-03.

Other critics claim that the funding mechanism of Social Security's pay-as-you-go funding mechanism has similarities with an illegal Ponzi scheme, where early investors are paid off out of funds collected from later investors instead of from profits from business activity.

The Social Security Administration responds to the criticism as follows:

> There is a superficial analogy between pyramid or Ponzi schemes and pay-as-you-go insurance programs in that in both money from later participants goes to pay the benefits of earlier participants. But that is where the similarity ends. A pay-as-you-go system can be visualized as a simple pipeline, with money from current contributors coming in the front end and money to current beneficiaries paid out the back end. As long as the amount of money coming in the front end of the pipe maintains a rough balance with the money paid out, the system can continue forever. There is no unsustainable progression driving the mechanism of a pay-as-you-go pension system, and so it is not a pyramid or Ponzi scheme. If the demographics of the population were stable, then a pay-as-you-go system would not have demographically-driven financing ups and downs, and no thoughtful person would be tempted to compare it to a Ponzi arrangement. However,

since population demographics tend to rise and fall, the balance in pay-as-you-go systems tends to rise and fall as well. This vulnerability to demographic ups and downs is one of the problems with pay-as-you-go financing. But this problem has nothing to do with Ponzi schemes or any other fraudulent form of financing; it is simply the nature of pay-as-you-go systems.[2]

So, no, Social Security cannot simply be dismissed as a Ponzi scheme.

How much are Social Security benefits increasing in 2023?

Approximately 70 million Americans will see an 8.7% increase in their Social Security benefits and Supplemental Security Income (SSI) payments in 2023. On average, Social Security benefits will increase by $146 per month starting in January.

Federal benefit rates increase when the cost-of-living rises, as measured by the Department of Labor's Consumer Price Index (CPI-W). The CPI-W rises when inflation increases, leading to a higher cost-of-living. This change means prices for goods and services, on average, are higher. The cost-of-

---

[2] Larry DeWitt, Historian's Office, "Research Note #25: Ponzi Schemes vs. Social Security," *Social Security Online*, U.S. Social Security Administration, January 2009. Retrieved 2009-03-17.

living adjustment (COLA) helps to offset these costs.

"Medicare premiums are going down and Social Security benefits are going up in 2023, which will give seniors more peace of mind and breathing room. This year's substantial Social Security cost-of-living adjustment is the first time in over a decade that Medicare premiums are not rising and shows that we can provide more support to older Americans who count on the benefits they have earned," said acting Commissioner Kilolo Kijakazi.

January 2023 marks when other changes will happen based on the increase in the national average wage index. For example, the maximum amount of earnings subject to Social Security payroll tax in 2023 will be higher, rising from $147,000 to $160,200. The retirement earnings test exempt amounts under full retirement age are increasing from $19,560 a year ($1,630 a month) to $21,240 a year ($1,770 a month). One dollar in benefits will be withheld for every $2 in earnings above the limit.

Do you lose benefits permanently if you keep working?

While Social Security does have a rule, called the "earnings limit" or "earning test," that can *temporarily* reduce the benefits of people who are still working, it does not apply to all working beneficiaries and it is not permanent.

The rule only covers people who claim benefits before full retirement age and continue working. In this circumstance, Social Security withholds a portion of benefits if earnings from work exceed a set cap, which changes every year and differs depending on how close you are to full retirement age.

In 2023, your benefits are reduced by $1 for every $2 in income above $21,240, if you won't hit full retirement age until a later year. If you will reach FRA in 2023, the formula is $1 less in benefits for every $3 in earnings above $56,520. In the month when you hit FRA, the earnings test goes away — there's no benefit reduction, regardless of your income. Social Security also adjusts your benefit upward so that over time, you will recoup the money that was withheld.

Do you pay taxes on Social Security benefits?

Yes, although that was not true until 1984. The Social Security overhaul passed by Congress and signed by President Ronald Reagan the year before included a provision that made *a portion* of Social Security benefit taxable, *depending* on your income level.

You will pay federal income tax on up to 50 percent of your benefits if your income for the year is $25,000 to $34,000 for an individual filer and $32,000 to $44,000 for a couple filing jointly. Above those thresholds, up to 85 percent of benefits are taxable. Below them, you do not owe the IRS anything on your benefits. In general terms, Social Security counts as income the money you get from work pensions and investments; nontaxable interest; and half of your Social Security benefits.

Additionally, you might also owe *state taxes* on your Social Security income if you live in Colorado, Connecticut, Kansas, Minnesota, Missouri, Montana, Nebraska, New Mexico, Rhode Island, Vermont, Utah or West Virginia. Of course, the rules on taxing benefits vary widely from state to state.

* * * * * * *

Now you have a basic understanding of the current system of Social Security, which means you know more than 90% of Americans about this subject and are in a much better position to debate reforming the system this semester.

NOTE: Some of the information here might be something you want to use for evidence. You cannot simply cite this handbook as evidence. You need to find that evidence from an online source, which is usually going to be from the Social Security Administration website. But if you have specific statistics that you are looking for, such as the amount that benefits went up in 2022 because of COLA, then you should be able to find a credible online source that you can use for acceptable evidence.

Chapter 3.
Social Security Reform

When we debate reforming Social Security, we are focusing specifically on the issue of keeping the system solvent. We are not talking about reforming the bureaucratic elements of the Social Security Administration or privatizing the system. At issue is how to ensure that your parents, you, your children, and your children's children will receive Social Security payments in the future, and that those payments will be substantial enough for each of you to live in retirement.

Therefore, any plan put forward by the Affirmative in these debates has to address keeping the system solvent.

Does Social Security need radical reform to stay solvent?

No, there is no need for radical reform. Relatively modest reforms can keep the system running for generations to come. It is true, that the ratio between taxpayers and payees was original 10:1 and now for several decades the ratio has been 3:1 and the system still worked.

However, because Baby Boomers are retiring at the rate of 10,000 per day, we are heading for a future where only two taxpayers will be supporting each retiree. That is important because the system does *not* work as it is currently structured at a 2:1 ratio.

Think about it. If you go from 3 to 2 taxpayers supporting a retiree, the amount of money in the pipeline for each retiree has been cut by a third. That would mean instead of getting roughly $1,500 a month, each retiree would be getting $1,000. How many people could live on $1,000 a month? Keep in mind that the poverty line for in 2023 is $1458 for an individual.

What can be done? There are two options. Either you pump more money into the pipeline, by raising revenues, or you cut back on the drainage on the other end of the pipe, usually by trimming benefits.

Let us look at the main options for each of those two choices.

How can we pump more money into the pipeline?

There are several ways of doing that.

- *Raise the Social Security payroll tax by ½ of 1%.* Be aware that the tax rate has not gone up in 40 years. Changes to the tax rate would affect all covered workers and would not change benefits. Increasing rates alone could close the entire solvency gap, and even a modest change, such as a gradual increase of 0.3 percentage points for employees and employers (or less than $3 per week for an average earner), could close about one-fifth of the gap.

- *Raise the payroll tax base.* Currently once you make over $147,000, you no longer pay Social Security taxes. Raising the cap would help mitigate the erosion of Social Security's payroll tax base caused by rising wage inequality. Most workers' taxes would not change, while the degree of increase in high earners' taxes would depend on whether the cap were raised or eliminated. Raising the tax cap could increase higher earners' benefits as well, depending on how policymakers treat newly taxed earnings. Changes to the tax cap could close roughly a quarter to nearly nine-tenth of Social Security's solvency gap, depending on how they were structured.

- *Tax all Social Security benefits.* Currently, only 50% to 85% of benefits are taxable. If your combined income is above a certain limit (the IRS calls this limit the base amount), you will need to pay at least some tax. The limit for 2023 is $25,000 if the person is a single filer, head of household or qualifying widow or widower with a dependent child. The 2023 limit for joint filers is $32,000. If they are married and file separately, they would likely have to pay taxes on their Social Security income. However, in 2022 there was a bill proposed by Rep. Angie Craig (D-MN) known as the You Earned It, You Keep It Act, which would make it so that the federal government takes *no* money from Social Security payments. To make up for the lost revenue, Craig proposed raising the cap on Social Security payroll taxes from $147,000 to $250,000.

- *Require more/all workers to pay into the system.* Many state and local government workers do not pay into Social Security. Who is exempt from paying into Social Security? Self-employed workers who make less than $400 annually do not pay Social Security taxes. All individuals are exempt from paying the tax on wages above a certain threshold. Members of certain religious groups are often exempt if they waive their rights to benefits, including hospital insurance benefits (they must be members of a religious sect that is conscientiously opposed to receiving private death and retirement benefits and provides food, shelter, and medical care for its members). Most foreign academics and researchers are exempt if they are nonimmigrant and nonresident aliens.

In terms of each of these proposals, you would need to know how much additional money is pumped into the system, so that you can argue that this is enough keep the system solvent.

How can we drain less money out of the pipeline?

Again, there are several ways of doing that.

- *Raise the retirement age.* Currently the program's full retirement age cuts off at age 67. Some advocate raising the age to 68, others to 70, and others split the different and want to raise it to 69. People are living longer and drawing benefits longer than anticipated when the law was enacted in 1935 when the average lifespan in the United States was 61 for men and 65 for women. Today, men are expected to live until 74.5 and women until 80.2. A proposal by a bipartisan group of U.S. senators, led by Angus King (Ind.-Maine) and Bill Cassidy (Rep-Louisiana), are among several efforts to overhaul Social Security. It would, among other things, increasing the age for receiving full benefits to 70. The proposal is expected to face stiff opposition in Congress and among senior advocacy groups. Retirees already receiving Social Security benefits probably would not be affected, while those who take benefits early would be impacted the most. It is unclear what may change for those who wait until 70 to get a bigger check. Retirement income planning would become even more critical for retirees.

- *Reduce future cost-of-living adjustments by ½ or 1%.* Many economists say that the current COLA formula is too generous.

- *Change the retirement formula to slightly reduce future benefits.* For about 50 years now retirement benefits have been based on the highest 35 years of earnings. Raising this to 38 years could result in slightly smaller benefits.

- *Slightly reduce benefits to wealthier retirees.* Currently, Social Security benefits are not means-tested.

Again, you would need numbers that would show reducing the payments would help to keep the system solvent. The Affirmative has to prove the plan will solve for the harms established in their constructive speech.

* * * * * * *

These are just eight suggestions out of hundred ideas, but they represent the main solutions that have been offered for which you will be able to find evidence.

One of the first things we will establish in this class is which of these eight suggestions will Affirmative teams be able to run. We need a limited number because Negatives need to be able to prepare responses to any possible Affirmative case. Having eight things to respond to is way too much. Can Affirmatives run more than one solution? Can they run one of each type? These are things we need to determine.

Note: In the back of this book there are four pages where you can write down exactly what has been cleared for harms, plan planks/solvency, Plan Attacks and Disadvantages.

Chapter 4.
Voting Issue

How do you *win* the round? Given all the arguments and evidence that make up the round, how do the judges—which means both the instructor grading the round as well as the students critiquing the round—determine who "wins" the round?

The decision of the judge is based on the voting issues in the round. None of the arguments and evidence in the round matter unless they impact one of the voting issues.

The Negative has presumption (things are the way they should be), and the Affirmative has the burden of proof (to justify change). Basically, the Affirmative has to win all—or at least most—of the voting issues in the round. The Negative can win the round by winning just *one* of the voting issues. There are not hard and fast rules, because it depends on the strength of the arguments and evidence in the round.

There are four voting issues in your debates. Two are raised by the Affirmative and two are raised by the Negative.

1. *Harms (Significance).* The Affirmative has to prove that there is one or more significant harms existing in the *status quo* that have to be addressed. Debaters talk about "harms" in the round, but they have to be "significant" harms, that justify changing the current system.

Significance can be qualitative and/or quantitative. Qualitative means that harms has a major impact on people: they become ill, they lose their homes, they end up dead. Quantitative means it impacts a major number of people.

For example, during Covid, there were people who argued against vaccinations because people suffered serious side effects. They got sick, they were unable to work, and a few died. Those are qualitative harms. But the number of people who were affected that way were statistically insignificant, both when compared to other vaccinations, and, more importantly, when compared to the hundreds of thousands of people who were dying from Covid. By that standard the harms are not quantitatively significant, and becoming ill or being unable to work because of the vaccine are not as qualitatively significant as dying from Covid.

Ideally, the Affirmative can have one evidence card that establishes both the harm an its significance, but often you will need one card to prove something is a harm and another card to prove it is significant.

Conversely, the Negative can argue that the Affirmative harms are not harms and/or they are not significant harms. Specifically this would mean arguing that Social Security is *not* becoming insolvent, or that the harm is relatively minor. With the latter the idea is that the major Disadvantages of enacting the plan would outweigh the minor harms because payments are reduced (of course, it would depend on the amount of the reductions).

2. Solvency. Once the Affirmative establishes that there is a significant harm in the *status quo*, then they have to show they can solve those significant harms. If the plan does not solve the harms, then why would the judge vote for the plan?

In this case, what the Affirmative needs to prove is that each specific plan to raise revenue or lower payments generates enough money or saves enough money to keep Social Security solvent.

Also, keep in mind that there will be a clash on what constitutes Social Security being solvent. Does that mean that the current payouts are maintained? Does that include adjustments for inflation? Or does it mean lower payouts in the future? Will those be sufficient for people on Social Security to live?

One of the things the Affirmative can argue is not that they totally solve the problem, because there will always be people who continue to be harmed for various reasons, but that the Affirmative offers a *comparative advantage* over the *status quo*. Given a choice between the current system and the Affirmative proposal, more people will be better off under the Affirmative plan.

You can anticipate that solvency will be the single most important issue in debate rounds this semester.

3. *Plan Attacks*. The flip side of solvency, where the Affirmative tries to prove their plan will solve the harms, are the Plan Attacks the Negative raises to reduce solvency. In practical terms, this means that for each of the options the Affirmative can use to increase the amount of money going into the system and/or decrease the amount of money being paid out of the system, the Negative has a Plan Attack for that specific option.

For example, the last year I debated in college the topic was consumer product safety and this was so long ago our Affirmative plan was to require airbags and lap belts in all cars. Having airbags and lap belts would save thousands of lives. Negatives would run a Plan Attack in which they pointed out that we would not be solving for cars that were (a) in collisions from the side or (b) accidents that involved multiple collisions. Both of those points are true, but those are insignificant numbers compared to the lives that would be saved. In other words, the plan had a comparative advantage over the *status quo*. Just because we did not save *everybody* did not take away from the plan saving *thousands* of lives more than the *status quo*.

4. *Disadvantages*. The other way for the Negative to attack the Affirmative plan is to argue that it will create *new* problems that are more significant than the harms for which the Affirmative is trying to solve. Yes, there is a weird aspect to this voting issue because after arguing that the Affirmative harms are not significant and the Affirmative cannot solve for those harms, the Negative now argues that IF the Affirmative plan is enacted, then it will create new problems.

So, basically, the Negative argues that even if the Affirmative is right, then the world will be worse than it was before.

In college debate, it seemed that anything the Affirmative plan did would result in global thermonuclear war. How? Simple. The government adopts the plan and this ticks off some nation that will respond aggressively in terms of economics, the trade war become a real war, any real war will go nuclear, and everybody on the planet dies.

Yes, it is a stupid argument, but there is evidence for each link. No, you are not allowed to run a global thermonuclear war Disadvantage.

Whereas Plan Attacks are specific to the provisions in the Affirmative plan, Disadvantages are more general. You should have at least one Disadvantage that you can run again any Affirmative that increases revenue for Social Security and at least one to run against cases that decrease the amount of benefits.

Again, this is something we will vote on to determine what limited number of Disadvantages the Negative can run in a round. This is because just as the Negative needs to know what the Affirmative can argue in terms of harms and solvency to be able to find evidence to run against, the Affirmative gets to know what specific Plan Attacks and Disadvantages the Negative can run to find evidence against those.

The Negative Disadvantage(s) are weighed against the Affirmative's solvency. It is possible that the judge could agree that the Affirmative solves the harms *and* creates the Disadvantage, but the Disadvantage does *not* outweigh the solvency of the harms.

In other words, it is debatable.

NEGATIVE STRATEGIES

There are various lines of attack that the Negative can take against the Affirmative plan. The Negative does not have to do *all* of these but they should do more than one.

1. They can argue that the harms are not harms. Students take out student loans to go to college. Going to college is a good thing. College graduates make more money than non-college graduates. How is this a bad thing?

2. They can argue that the harms are not significant. In other words, there are people who are being hurt, but there is not a significant number of them. Certainly not enough to vote for the Affirmative plan. One year we were debating global warming and the argument was that the alkaline level of seas water is going up. If this happens the food chain is imperiled for the entire planet. One of the Negatives found that the increase each *century* was ridiculously low, so it would take hundreds if not thousands of years to become a significant problem. That was a killer card. Everybody got it to run on Negative and the Affirmatives stopped running that as a harm.

3. The Negative can argue that the plan will not solve the problem. Now, the Affirmative rarely wants to argue that they can solve the problem for *everybody*, but that there have a *comparative advantage* over the *status quo*. If there are not Disadvantages or Plan Attacks that outweigh the Solvency, they we should vote to adopt the Affirmative plan.

Solvency is where the Negative can make *alternative causality* arguments. Yes, it is a problem. Yes, it is a significant problem, but you cannot solve for it because there are other causes. Students do not just get student loans to pay for college. They use it for rent, for buying a car, for going to Florida on Spring Break. You give them free public college tuition and they will keep getting in debt (lots of evidence on Credit Card debt can be raised).

The Negative can also attack Solvency in terms of Plan Attacks. These are problems with the Affirmative plan planks that will affect solvency. For example, the federal government is inherently inefficient, which means the plan will waste money, or the administration will force the Social Security Administration to hire more people to make this work, but the Affirmative does not do that so the system will fail.

What is the difference between a Negative Solvency attack and a Plan Attack? The former argues that the Affirmative's Solvency evidence is wrong. It responds to what the Affirmative argued in its Constructive speech. The latter brings up other concerns about Solvency that the Affirmative did not talk about. This is where alternative causality can come into play, because there are other factors that cause the problem. Since the

Affirmative does not solve for those other factors, they cannot solve the harms.

4. The Negative can argue that reforming Social Security will create Disadvantages, which are significant *new* problems that do not exist with the current system. For example, if you raise taxes to keep Social Security payments the same, that will have economic impacts that will be harmful.

The Negative, in theory, has to win only ONE of these Voting Issues to win the round. But there is no reason not to launch all four lines of attack in the Negative Constructive speech and then deciding which are the ones to emphasize in the Negative Rebuttal.

Chapter 5.
Debate Format

A debate consists of two sides. In policy debate there are two debaters on each side, constituting a debate team, but in this class, we are doing a variation of the Lincoln-Douglas format, which means one debater on each side.

For this semester our topic is Social Security and our resolution is as follows:

> *Resolved: That that the United States should significantly reform Social Security.*

<u>You cannot change the wording of this resolution</u>. Everybody uses the same resolution in their Affirmative Constructive.

To make sure the Negative can prepare for these debates, we will limit the numbers of harms and plan planks that Affirmatives can advance in their constructive speeches.

The specific topic areas and the specific plan planks means that the Negative knows what the Affirmative team might run and can prepare responses for each topic and planks. Your initial assignments will be gathering Affirmative and Negative evidence for each topic and plan area.

The Affirmative take the "pro" side supporting the resolution, while the Negative takes the "con" side against the resolution. Affirmative argues to adopt the resolution by offering a plan to significantly address the problem of Social Security remaining solvent, while the Negative argues to maintain the *status quo* (the current system).

The Affirmative gives three speeches in the round, while the Negative gives two. The Affirmative gives both the first and last speech in the round, just like the prosecution does in a court trial. This is because the Affirmative has the burden of proof. Even though one side has three speeches and the other two, the speeches on both sides add up to 13 minutes each.

NOTE: At this point you might be struck by the fact that you will be speaking longer in a debate than you did in any one speech you gave in your Public Speaking class. This is true. But keep in mind that in the constructive speeches over half the time will be spent signposting your points and reading evidence. Your signposting is laid out on your flow sheet. The evidence is on cards that you read aloud. It is only when you argue the warrants, and explain how that argument wins you a voting issue that you look at the audience and speak extemporaneously.

Each speaker gives two types of speeches during the debate, a longer one (6 or 8 minutes) called a constructive speech and a shorter one (3, 4 or 5 minutes) called a rebuttal.   Speeches become shorter because arguments become more focused as the debate proceeds. A case might be based on six arguments, but the round might come down to just two or three of those six arguments as it impact the voting issues.

Additionally, the debate is broken down into two main areas: case side (harms and solvency) and plan side (Plan Attacks and Disadvantages).

SPEECH BREAKDOWN

Here are the speeches that make up a round. They total 40 minutes, which gives us time to critique the round afterwards in a 50-minute class period:

Speech	Speaker	Time (minutes)
Affirmative Constructive	Affirmative (Case Side: Harms, Solvency)	6
Cross-Examination	Affirmative by Negative	3
Prep Time	Negative	2
Negative Constructive	Negative (Plan Side: Plan Attacks, Disadvantages, Case Side: Harms, Solvency)	8

Cross-Examination	Negative by Affirmative	3
Prep Time	Affirmative	2
First Affirmative Rebuttal	Affirmative (Case Side: Harms, responding to the Negative's responses to the Affirmative case, and to the Negative's Plan Attacks)	4
Prep Time	Negative	2
Negative Rebuttal	Negative responds to the First Affirmative Rebuttal	5
Prep Time	Affirmative	2
Second Affirmative Rebuttal	Affirmative responds to the Negative Rebuttal	3
Speech	**Speaker**	**Time (40 minutes)**

For example, the "Pro" debate begins with the Affirmative Constructive speech laying out the case, establishing significant harms that establish a need for change in a six-minute speech. They are then cross-examined (questioned) for 3 minutes by the Negative speaker.

Then the Negative has two minutes of prep time before they give their speech (Each speaker has two minutes of prep time before their speech and the prep time always comes *after* the cross-examination of the constructive speech).

The Negative Constructive argues against the case laid out in Affirmative constructive in an eight-minute speech and then they are cross-examined for 3 minutes by the Affirmative. You will notice that the Negative Constructive is two minutes longer than the Affirmative Constructive. That is because in addition to responding to what the Affirmative argued in terms of harms and solvency, the Negative is also raising new arguments in terms of Plan Attacks and Disadvantages.

The First Affirmative Rebuttal responds to the Negative's attacks on the harms and solvency, and the Negative Plan Attacks. In other words, it responds to everything argued by the Negative (and extends anything that the Negative dropped in the Affirmative case). This is a four-minute speech responding to an eight-minute speech, so the Affirmative has to focus more on the key clashes in the round and not try to cover everything, because there is simply not enough time.

The Negative Rebuttal responds to the First Affirmative Rebuttal. This is a five-minute speech, so the Negative is responding to everything that the Affirmative just covered in its First Rebuttal plus whatever the Affirmative dropped that the Negative thinks can help them win the round.

The Second Affirmative Rebuttal responds to the Negative Rebuttal. In this three-minute speech you are not covering anything, but focusing on the key clash for each voting issue and arguing why you win it and the round.

After we talk about evidence in the next chapter, there will be three chapters dealing with the Affirmative Constructive, the Negative Constructive, and all three Rebuttals. So this section is just providing a general introduction.

Each of your speeches are graded separately, along with both CX periods. So the Affirmative receives five grades and the Negative four grades at the end of the debate.

USE ALL OF YOUR SPEAKING TIME

At this point let me underscore that you should be using all of your speaking and cross-examination time throughout the round. You should be able to see the timer that I have set up on my laptop, but you should also be using the timer on your phone to make sure you always know how much time you have left in your speech. You have way more arguments and evidence than you can ever use in any given speech, so there is no excuse for being short on time.

There are penalties for being significantly short on time. If you were a minute short, that would be at least a one grade penalty.

But also, if you have a minute left, then you should at the very least be able to stand there, look at us, and build your ballot. Underscore what voting issues you have won.

Bottom line: Use all of your speaking time.

P.S. Yes, there are penalties for going *over* time as well. The rule is simple. When the clock gets to zero you should finish the sentence you are saying. After that, I stop flowing. Anything else you say does not count. So why keep talking?

BUILDING THE AFFIRMATIVE CASE

The first 5-minute Affirmative Constructive speech has the following structure:

- Observation
- Resolution
- Harms
- Plan
- Solvency

Observation: Each side begins with a basic observation. This is either a fact (or set of facts) and/or a philosophical statement that sets up the resolution. This could be something about the number of economists who argue the threat to Social Security's solvency is a serious problem or an expert talking about how we are running out of time to deal with the problem.

Resolution: This is where the resolution for the semester is stated. The Affirmative says, "*Resolved: That that the United States should significantly reform Social Security*." NOTE: In a 6-minute speech you want to spend around 30 seconds on the observation and resolution, so you have over 5-minutes to cover harms, the plan, and solvency.

Harms: The Affirmative establishes the problems with the *status quo* that need to be changed and which can only be solved with the adoption of the Affirmative plan. These should be significant problems (otherwise, why change anything?). The assumption is that you will develop at least two or three significant harms (because you do not want to put all of your argumentative eggs in one basket) with corresponding solvency points.

Plan: In a minimum number of sentences the Affirmative states what the government should do to significantly reform Social Security. That means which of the options for pumping more money into the pipeline and/or draining less money out of the pipeline are being advocated by the Affirmative? You will be using more than one, but you will not be using all of them. There is not enough time to prove solvency for all of them in the constructive speech.

Since only the Affirmative is arguing to change the current system, they are the only side that has to establish a plan (the Negative is defending the *status quo*, so they do not need a plan).

Note: the Affirmative has what is called fiat power, which means that for the sake of argument (i.e., this debate), that the plan is automatically enacted. The fact that Congress would never pass it and that President Trump would veto any such legislation (assuming either of these statements is true) does not matter. The debate is about whether the problems are significant and if the Affirmative plan can solve those problems without causing additional significant problems.

Solvency: Once the Affirmative establishes specific problems, it needs to argue how the Affirmative plan solves those exact same problems. That means for *each* plank in the plan, you have a solvency card that will argue how that element helps to reduce the harms established earlier in the speech.

Contention I consists of Harms sub-points A and B (and possibly C), while Contention 2 Solvency has parallel sub-points A and B (and possibly C), meaning that 2A solves the harms of 1A, 2B solves the harms of 1B, etc. Everybody should be consistent on their signposting.

Chapter 6.
Evidence Cards

Because you do not have the ability to advance an argument on your own authority--you are not an expert on Social Security--you need evidence to support your claims.

TYPES OF EVIDENCE

There are four general categories of evidence, each of which includes specific types of evidence.

Examples

Because you are debating a real-world issue, examples drawn from the real world will be key evidence in making your argument.

1. *Factual Illustration*: A real world example provided with specific details that flesh it out.

2. *Hypothetical Illustration*: This is a "what if" type of example, where it is something that *might* happen. This type of illustration is comparatively week because it is hypothetical; factual illustrations will always be stronger.

3. *Specific Instance*: A specific case provided without details. The Golden Gate Bridge is an example of a suspension bridge. You do not provide any details, the way you would with a factual illustration, because it is assumed the audience understands the reference.

4. *Definition:* A statement of the exact meaning of a word, usually coming form a dictionary, such as a definition of the term "solvency."

An effective argumentative technique is to combine a factual illustration with one or more specific instances. For example, you can talk about the importance of military alliances using World War II as your factual illustration, providing appropriate details, and then reference World War I, the Korean War, etc., as specific instances that show there are plenty of other examples to support your claim.

Analogies

Not always considered a type of evidence, the argumentative power of analogy is that if you can convince an audience that "A" is just like "B," then you can argue similar results, good or bad.

4. *Literal Analogy*: Comparing two things from the real world, such as comparing the War on Terror with the Vietnam War or World War II. Example: the topic is providing free tuition

for public colleges in the U.S. The Affirmative wants to prove this will work by citing what happens in other nations that provide free college tuition.

5. *Figurative Analogy*: Comparing something in the real world to something that is not literally true, such as calling Donald Trump a bull in a china shop. The president is not literally a bull nor is he in a china shop, but an audience could buy the idea Trump is like a bull and that his actions and policies might do serious damage. Then again, they might not buy it.

Testimony

Sometimes called "Expert Testimony" because while it might be assumed that testimony being cited is from an expert, that is not necessarily the case. The distinction between the two types of Testimony is based on <u>how</u> the evidence is presented.

6. *Quotation*: Providing the exact words of the source, quoting them verbatim (and not omitting words that alter the meaning of the quotation).

7. *Paraphrase*: Putting the source's position into your own words. You would rarely do this when you present evidence in a debate

round, although when you refer back to a quotation in a later speech you can certainly paraphrase it at that point in the round.

<u>Statistics</u>

Numbers are used to quantify evidence and as such there are two different types of numbers to be found in statistical evidence:

8. *Descriptive Statistic*: These are statistics in which you count all of something.   For example, in the wake of an election, we have the exact number of votes each candidate received.

9. *Inferential Statistic*: These are statistics where you take a sampling and extrapolate the meaning and significance to the general population.   For example, before the election, polls are taken of registered voters trying to predict what the vote will be. Whereas the election returns count <u>all</u> the actual voters, polls count only a small fraction of the actual voters.

One of the requirements you will have for your Constructive speeches is that you use multiple types of evidence to establish an argument. For example, you can combine a quotation from an expert with inferential statistics or combine a factual illustration with descriptive statistics to create a stronger argument.   A story about someone who lost their home because of rising water levels caused by melting arctic ice would bring a human impact to the statistical data on that subject.

HOW TO SEARCH FOR EVIDENCE ON THE INTERNET

In the 21st century you will probably be finding all of your evidence online. There are certainly books and magazines articles about reforming Social Security that you can find at the UMD Library, but the information in those books might be outdated and you would end up having to search data bases to find the articles you need. So looking online is key.

The evidence you need is out there. The question is *how* to find it. Here are some helpful hints to make you searches for evidence more efficient and more successful.

1. *Be Specific.* The more relevant words you use in any search, the more successful your results will be. Typing just "Social Security" is too broad and will provide too many unnecessary results. But typing "Tax all Social Security benefits" will get you to sources that talk specifically about that plan plank.

2. *Use Quotes to Search for a Phrase.* When you do a search, you can use quotation marks to group words together. This tells the search engine that everything inside the quotes should be grouped just like that in the results. Using quotes will drastically

cut down the number of results the search engine shows you. For example, you could type "Social Security" and "raise retirement age," to narrow the focus on your search.

3. *Restrict Your Searches to Specific Domains.* This is specific to Google, where there is a "site" option. For example, you could search for information about Social Security at a specific site, such as "site:forbes.com" or a particular top-level domain, such as "site:gov" to provide information just from those sites.

4. *Use Addition and Subtraction to Make Search Results More Relevant.* You can also do a Boolean search, where you tell the search engine to ignore things. The classic example of this is if you were looking for "Tom Ford" and kept getting lots of results for the Ford Motor Company, then you would say "Tom Ford" -motors, which would get rid of all the results about the car company.

5. *Run a Wildcard Search.* With most search engines you can use a wildcard character, such as the asterisk (*), hashtag (#), or question mark (?), to throw a broader search net. This tells the search engine that it can replaced the wildcard character with whatever it finds (the asterisk is the most common wildcard character). So you would search for "Social security * reform" and see what shows up.

6. *Try Multiple Search Engines*. Do not fall into the trap of using just one search engine for all of your web searches. Just because "googling something" suggests using the Google search engine there are others out there. Bing, Yahoo, Startpage. Com, Yandex, Ask.com and DuckDuckGo are the other main ones. So if one search engine is not helping you find what you are looking for, you should try one or two of the others to see if that gets you better results. After all, each search engine has different algorithms and unique filtering options that can provide you different results.

7. *Search a Web Site for a Specific Word*. When you start searching your results and land on a particular page, you might still have a problem finding what you were looking for. Every web browser lets you do a keyword search on any given web page. You just hit Control+F for Windows or Command+F for Mac as the keyboard shortcut that gets you the prompt asking you what you are looking for.

P.S. If you have having trouble finding specific evidence you need (e.g., what the Affirmative would run against one of the Disads the Negative would run against their case), you can also email your instructor. You will not be given actually evidence or a specific website, but you will get suggestions on how to conduct the search (that means that I searched the web until I found a source with good evidence and that I will tell you what I searched for but not what I found, so that you can then go and search for it and find it yourself.

EVIDENCE FORMAT

You need to format your evidence correctly so that you can use it in a round. That means *all* of your cards need to follow the same format.

Traditionally, evidence goes on index cards because they are easier to organize, both before and during the round. Far easier than having them on half sheets of paper, or having them on your computer. Index cards come in three basic sizes: 3 x 5, 4 x 6 and 5 x 8. Of those 4 x 6 is the optimal size because you would have to make the print really small to cut and paste your evidence on to 3 x 5 cards. You can also get index cards in different colors, so you can color code evidence: yellow is harms, red is solvency, etc. Because you cut and paste the evidence on to the cards you will need a glue stick or lots of scotch tape to put your cards together.

There are three sections to each card: (1) tag, (2) source, and (3) quotation. On each card there are spaces between each section. Here is a sample card based on evidence from a previous chapter where you can see the three parts are clearly delineated:

SS Trust Fund has other benefits AFF HARM

William G. Shipman, co-chairman, "Retiring with Dignity: Social Security vs. Private Markets," *Cato Project on Social Security*, August 14, 1995.

In common usage a trust fund is an estate of money and securities held in trust for its beneficiaries. The Social Security Trust Fund is quite different. It is an accounting of the difference between tax and benefit flows. When taxes exceed benefits, the federal government lends itself the excess in return for an interest-paying bond, an IOU that it issues to itself. The government then spends its new funds on unrelated projects such as bridge repairs, defense, or food stamps. The funds are not invested for the benefit of present or future retirees.

1.   *The Tag*. The tag is always only one line long. Anything longer and it becomes difficult to write down the entire tag during the round. The "tag" is the claim being made by the quotation (make sure the claim fits the actual evidence).

Each card should have its own unique tag. You are not going to need two cards that make the exact same point, although certainly you can have cards that you can use to extend a point (e.g., you have a study that proves X and you have an extension card to use in your rebuttal that has another study that also proves X).

The tag is in boldface so it stands out as such (you can also put it in all-CAPS). In addition to the claim, there are indications as to which side and which voting issue the card can be used to argue in a round.

This helps you to keep your cards organized. For the side it is either AFF or NEG. There are no other options. For the voting issue you could have HARM, SIGN, SOLV, P.A., or D.A. because the only things you can argue in a round are harms, significance (of the harms), solvency, Plan Attack, and Disadvantages.

You can also indicate on each card which specific harms/solvency area or Plan Attack/Disadvantage, each card applies to. Say you are the Negative and you know there are five possible plan elements the Affirmative can run in the round. So you have your Plan Attacks and Disadvantages grouped by the those five. When you learn which two or three the Affirmative is running, you keep those piles, and put the others away because you will not need them.

Everything you do to prepare your cards to be used in a round decreases the amount of time you need in the round to find the right cards and the more prep time you are giving yourself during the round.

2. *Source.* For each card you need to provide the following to identify the sources: (a) the name of the source, (b) their credentials, (c) the title of the piece, (d) the "publisher" of the piece, and (e) the date it was "published." So in the example above,

(a) William G. Shipman is (b) the co-chairman of the Cato Project on Social Security, who wrote (c) "Retiring with Dignity: Social Security vs. Private Marks," which was found on the website (d) *Cato Project on Social Security*, and (e) first posted on August 14, 1995.

3. *Quotation*. The actual evidence. You provide a direct quotation. You do *not* paraphrase the information and put it in your own words. You do not get to do that. You have to quote exactly what they say in their own words.

Recognize that you might have to edit a quotation (there could be some extraneous stuff in the middle of the quotation you need to cut and replace with . . . to show that something has been omitted).

How long should a quotation be? There is not an absolute rule, but let us say 2-5 sentences. You do not want a lot of one sentence quotations as evidence. It is hard to prove any point worth making in a single sentences. On the other hand, you do not want a quotation that goes on and on and on. Especially if it makes a whole bunch of points that you want to have as separate arguments on the flow.

WARRANT

In theory, you can use any conceivable piece of evidence for any given claim. To support the idea of addressing climate change you could point to the success of movies about Marvel superheroes. But what does that have to do with climate change? Nothing. It is <u>not</u> *good* evidence, because it does not *warrant* the claim.

The Warrant in an argument is simply the explanation for how the evidence supports the claim. If you cannot make the connection, then there is no reason for the audience to accept the argument (something your opponent will be only too happy to point out).

This means that you need all three parts—claim, evidence, and warrant—to have a complete argument. Your evidence cards have the claim (*tag*) and the evidence (*quotation*), so you just read those in the round. But you will need to argue out the warrant and explain how the evidence proves the point you are trying to make about a voting issue in the round.

You do not just read as many cards as you can in your speech. You argue how the evidence proves your point to win the voting issue and the round.

THE MAGIC FORMULA

Basically, every time you make an argument in a debate round you do the same five things in the exact same order every single time:

1. Signpost
2. Make a claim (the tag on the evidence card).
3. Provide evidence (the quotation on the evidence card or your reasoning in support of the claim).
4. Provide the warrant, explaining how the evidence proves your just read proves the claim you made.
5. Argue what this means for a voting issue in the round.

The (1) comes from your flow, the (2) and (3) come from the evidence card, and then you look at the audience and argue out the (4) and (5). Those last two are important, not just for being able to win the round, but because you have to get to *both* the warrant and the voting issues to justify getting a grade better than "C" on your speeches.

So while you read (1), (2) and (3) off your flow and evidence cards, (4) and (5) are where you look at your audience and argue out how your evidence proves your claim and how that argument wins you the voting issue and ultimately the round.

* * * * * *

The rest of this chapter has sample evidence cards on some basic points about this topic, formatted correctly so you have multiple examples of what you are trying to do. If your cards are not formatted correctly, then you are not going to get them cleared to use in a round, and if you do not have cleared cards then you cannot even debate in a round.

These are cards that you can use in a debate round, but they are very simple cards and most of them are outdated.

There are better ones out there.

Social Security is not fully funded   AFF HARM

Louise Gaille, Economist. "14 Chief Pros and Cons of Social Security," *Vittana.org, Personal Finance Blog,* August 16, 2018.

By 2028, the number of people claiming benefits through Social Security are expected to exceed the number of people paying into it. Some estimates have this event occurring as early as 2022. Although a good portion of the national debt in the U.S. is to the Social Security program through Treasury securities, redeeming those securities requires funds. That may result in higher tax rates, a larger federal deficit, or other financial consequences.

Claiming SS at 62 reduces payouts   AFF HARM

Christy Bieber, Personal Finance Writer, "Here Are the Pros and Cons of Claiming Social Security at Age 62," *The Motley Fool,* July 8, 2020.

Although there's clearly a case to be made for starting your benefits ASAP, there are also some downsides. Some of the biggest Disadvantages include: You'll permanently reduce the size of your check: Benefits could be reduced by as much as 30% compared with retiring at full retirement age, and all future cost-of-living increases will be based on a smaller starting benefit.

Ratio of covered works is now 2.8:1   AFF HARM

Social Security Administration, "Frequently Asked Questions: Ratio of Covered Workers to Beneficiaries," ssa.gov, accessed August 17,2 015.

In 1940, the payroll tax contributions of 159 workers paid for the benefits of one recipient. In 2013 the estimated ratio was 2.8 workers to each recipient.

Only 85% of benefit are taxed   AFF SOLV

Kelly C. Long, personal financial coach, "The pros and cons of delaying Social Security," *Journal of Accountancy*, March 31, 2022.

While Social Security becomes taxable once your total income exceeds the annual limit, even at its highest inclusion in taxable income, only 85% of the benefit is taxed. This means that if you delay Social Security while spending down pretax retirement accounts throughout your 60s, you'll likely be reducing your future required minimum distributions (RMDs), which are 100% taxable, and replacing that income in your 70s and beyond with lower-taxed Social Security benefits.

Reduce benefits for high earners   AFF SOLV

Lorie Konish, reporter covering personal finance, "7 changes Americans are willing to make to fix Social Security,' *CNBC*, August 3, 2022.

Wealthier retirees generally receive more generous benefits, even though they likely have more ways to fund their retirements, such as through pensions and savings. Means testing benefits for those with certain wealth or income could be another way to help reduce the program's shortfall.

Reducing benefits reduces shortfall   AFF SOLV

Lorie Konish, reporter covering personal finance, "7 changes Americans are willing to make to fix Social Security,' *CNBC*, August 3, 2022.

This would reduce the amount of benefits the top 20% of earners receive, and would reduce the shortfall by 11%.

Note: If you read more than one piece of evidence form the same source in a speech, then after the first time you would just say, "Lorie Konish, previously cited."

SS is Not Going Bankrupt   NEG HARM

Taylor Tepper, Forbes Advisor Staff, "No, Social Security Isn't Going Bankrupt," *Forbes Advisor*, February 13, 2023.

Social Security is not going bankrupt. Millennials will get many plenty of checks when they retire. If history is any guide, Social Security will likely be the most important source of retirement income when today's workers hang up their spurs.

Reducing SS Benefits would hurt   NEG SOLV

Maurice Backman, "How Much Money Will You Lose if Social Security Benefits Are Cut?" *The Motley Fool*, September 8, 2021.

Now, say your earnings statement estimates your monthly benefit at full retirement age at $1,600. That's just a touch more than what the average senior on Social Security collects today. Since the Social Security Trustees anticipate a 22% reduction in benefits, that means that instead of collecting $1,600 a month, you'll be in line for $1,248 instead. Or, to put it another way, you'll lose $352 a month, or $4,224 a year. Clearly, that's a fair amount of money.

Cutting SS Benefits is not popular   NEG PA

Sean Williams, Investment Planning reporter, "Here's What 'Cutting' Social Security Benefits Actually Means," *The Motley Fool*, August 11, 2019.

The idea of directly cutting Social Security payouts tends to be *extremely* unpopular among the public. This would involve reducing benefits across the board when the program runs out of its asset reserves in 2035. Back in 2014, the *Washington Post* created an informal online poll that allowed users to pick from one dozen "fixes" for Social Security, half of which focused on adding new revenue and half of which cut long-term expenditures. Users were free to choose as many of the solutions as they wanted, as long as they could honestly say they stood behind them.

People do not support benefit cuts   NEG PA

Sean Williams, Investment Planning reporter, "Here's What 'Cutting' Social Security Benefits Actually Means," *The Motley Fool*, August 11, 2019.

Of the 12 choices, doing nothing and simply cutting benefits when the program ran out of cash in roughly two decades' time finished dead last in the polling with about 2% support.

Fears create Negative Feedback Loop   NEG DA

Taylor Tepper, Forbes Advisor Staff, "No, Social Security Isn't Going Bankrupt," *Forbes Advisor*, February 13, 2023.

The problem with doom-and-glooming Social Security's future is that it can create a Negative feedback loop. If that essential program will ultimately recede, thus taking a big chunk of your wealth with it, what's the point of saving more now when you'll never have enough saved for later anyway? Why not just spend your savings on things that will bring you immediate joy? A clear-eyed understanding of Social Security's issues, then, can encourage you to save more now.

Social Security Tax Hikes would hurt   NEG DA

Maurice Backman, "Think Biden's Social Security Tax Hike Sounds Bad? Some Lawmakers Are Calling for Even More Extreme Measures?" *The Motley Fool*, October 3, 2022.

Earlier this year, Senators Bernie Sanders and Elizabeth Warren introduced legislation designed to shore up Social Security's finances and prevent benefit cuts. But to achieve that goal, their proposal seeks to reintroduce Social Security taxes on income above $250,000 a year, not $400,000. Furthermore, those taxes wouldn't just apply to income from a job -- they'd also apply to capital gains.

Chapter 7.
Affirmative Constructive

A Debate Round begins with the Affirmative Constructive speech. This speech is 6 minutes long and presents the Affirmative case.

The Affirmative Constructive has five specific elements:

1. Observation
2. Resolution
3. Harms
4. Plan
5. Solvency

Let us briefly look at what each of these five elements consists of, so you understand what role each plays in building the case.

1. *Observation*. The Affirmative begins with an opening point about the topic. It sets up the significance, the reason why it is worth debating Social Security. The Observation does *not* make a point that properly belongs under Harms or Solvency.

For this topic it would be possible for the Observation to have evidence about when it is predicted that Social Security will become insolvent, or how the government is doing nothing about fixing the problem, or how people count on Social Security being there when they retire.

2. *Resolution*. This is simply reading the resolution exactly as it appears in this handbook. You simply say: "Therefore I stand, Resolved: *That the United States should significantly reform Social Security*." That is it. Nothing else needs to be said.

3. *Harms*. This is the first of the two major building blocks for the Affirmative case. You could up with multiple reasons as to how and why people would be harmed if the Social Security system becomes insolvent. You would want the number of people affected and/or how they are affected to be significant.

You want multiple reasons because you want to avoid putting all of your eggs in one basket. The idea is that you argue each specific harm is an independent justification for voting Affirmative. In other words, you argue three harms and say any one of them, in and of itself, is sufficient reason to vote Affirmative.

4. *Plan*. This is a brief section in which you say which specific planks make up the Affirmative plan. You will have five options, give or take one, that you can use, but you will not have enough time to argue all five of them with evidence in Solvency. So you will need to select 2 or 3 and tell us what they are.

5. *Solvency.* The second of the two major building blocks for the Affirmative case. This is why you prove, with evidence, how each of the plan planks will solve the problem. If it is a plank that should increase revenue, then you need to prove it will raise sufficient revenue. If it is a plank that will reduce payouts, then you need to prove it will do that. Altogether, you need to be able to prove that Social Security will remain solvent in the future because of the cumulative effects of your plan planks.

* * * * * * *

What follows is a sample Affirmative Constructive speech for last year's topic that I delivered to the class as an example. All of the evidence is completely made up, because the point is to give you a sense of what a speech looks like (in terms of the evidence cards) and then how it sounds like (in terms of how you argue off of the cards.

So the pages on the left will be the outline from the flow and all of the evidence cards, while the pages on the right will have the speech given off of the cards. That way you can see the difference between what is on the outline and the cards and what a debater actually argues in a round.

OBSERVATION: A COLLEGE EDUCATION IS A MAGIC BULLET

Jeff Anderson, President Humbolt University, "Yes, Everyone Should Go to College," *The New York Times*, April 1, 2022.

The benefits of a college education are numerous. On average you make 27% more than those who do not go to college, live almost 5 years longer, and have less children, who you can afford to send to college.

Resolved: *That the United States should make public college tuition-free.*

We begin with the Observation that A College Education is a Magic Bullet." Jeff Anderson, President Humbolt University, "Yes, Everyone Should Go to College," *The New York Time*, April 1, 2022. "The benefits of a college education are numerous. On average you make 27% more than those who do not go to college, live almost 5 years long, and have less children, who you can afford to send to college."

Unfortunately, many Americans cannot afford to go to college, therefore I stand Resolved: *"That the United State should make public college tuition-free.*

CONTENTION I: FREE TUITION ALLOWS MORE AMERICANS TO GET COLLEGE DEGREES

A.   HARMS

1. HIGH TUITION STOPS MANY AMERICANS FROM GOING TO COLLEGE

Cynthia Sykes, Education Reporter, "Less People are Able to Afford College," *Akron Register-Digest*, February 14, 2022.

For more and more Americans, going to college is no longer an option because the costs are two high. The Average cost of tuition for four years of college is now $56,000, up 16% in the last decade. Many who end up going are only able to do so because they get scholarships, taking out student loans that will cripple them with debt, or get jobs while taking classes. And most end up doing more than one of those three options.

I advance my case with two independent contentions.

Contention I. Free Tuition Allows More Americans to Get College Degrees."

A. Harms.

My first point is that High Tuition Stops Many Americans From Going to College." Cynthia Sykes, Education Reporter, "Less People are Able to Afford College," *Akron Register-Digest,* February 14, 2022. "For more and more Americans, going to college is no longer an option because the costs are too high. The average cost of tuition for four years of college is now $56,000, up 16% in the last decade. Many who end up going are only able to do so because they get scholarships, taking out student loans that will cripple them with debt, or get jobs while taking classes. And most end up doing more than one of those three options."

So, not only is this a harm, it getting worse, because the cost of college keeps going up and up.

However, that is not the only problem that exists in the *status quo.*

2. HIGH TUITION IS THE MAIN REASON FOR NOT GOING TO COLLEGE

Robert Wayne, Economics Professor, Wake Forrest, "The Effects of Income Disparity on College Choices," Cincinnati Journal of Statistics, March 21, 2020.

Numerous surveys produce the same results. Looking at American without college degrees, 44% never went to college because the cost was prohibited while an additional 12% started college but dropped out because of high tuition. Another 3% failed because of bad grades. 21% went because they did not need college to get a job in their chosen field and 20% already had jobs.

PLAN: The United States will provide free tuition for American students attending American public colleges.

My second Harms point is that High Tuition is the Main Reason for Not Going to College. Robert Wayne, Economics Professor, Wake Forrest, "The Effects of Income Disparity on College Choices," *Cincinnati Journal of Statistics,* March 21, 2020. "Numerous surveys produce the same results. Looking at American without college degrees, 44% never went to college because the cost was prohibited while an additional 12% started college but dropped out because of high tuition. Another 3% failed because of bad grades. 21% went because they did not need college to get a job in their chosen field and 20% already had jobs."

That 44% of the Americans who did not go to college were stopped by the high cost of tuitions is absolutely a significant Harm. Fortunately, we can do something about this.

The Affirmative plan is for the United States to provide free tuition for American students attending American public colleges.

B. SOLVENCY

FREE COLLEGE TUITION REMOVES A SIGNIFICANT BARRIER TO ATTENDING COLLEGE

Beth Harmon, Secretary of Education, "What is the Future of Education in the United States?" *Forbes*, November 4, 2021.

Obviously, providing free college tuition would make it easier for many Americans to not only go to college but complete their degrees. The question is whether we, as citizens, are willing to support the education of our students not just through high school but on through college, the way many industrial nations are already doing.

B. Solvency. Free College Tuition Removes a Significant Barrier to Attending College. Beth Harmon, Secretary of Education, "What is the Future of Education in the United States?" *Forbes*, November 4, 2021. "Obviously, providing free college tuition would make it easier for many Americans to not only go to college but complete their degrees. The question is whether we, as citizens, are willing to support the education of our students not just through high school but on through college, the way many industrial nations are already doing."

The United States is not leading the world when it comes to free college tuition, and we should be because of all the benefits that comes with education both to individuals and to the nation.

In my speech, I have demonstrated two significant harms in the *status quo* and shown that the Affirmative plan will indeed solve those harms. That is why at the end of this round you should vote Affirmative.

I stand open for cross-examination.

* * * * * * *

Now you can see how the outline on your flow, that has the main point and the signposting, combined with the evidence on your cards, is turned into an actual speech in the round.

Early in the semester I will do a practice debate using the Social Security topic—also with completely made -up evidence—so that you can practice flowing a round for the first time. But this will give you another example of not only an Affirmative constructive speech, but the other four speeches in a round.

Chapter 8.
Negative Constructive

The Negative Constructive is 8 minutes long and comes after the Affirmative Constructive, the CX (cross-examination) of the Affirmative by the Negative, and the 2 minutes of prep time the Negative has at that point.

There are five elements that must be included in the Negative Constructive speech. However, unlike the Affirmative Constructive, the order of the elements is not set in stone.

1. Negative Philosophy
2. Response to Harms
3. Response to Solvency
4. Plan Attack(s)
5. Disadvantage(s)

After the Negative Philosophy, the choice is what does the Negative cover first: case side (2 & 3) or plan side (4 & 5). The advantage to doing case side first is that it pairs the responses to solvency with the Plan Attacks, both of which go after the voting issue of solvency. The difference? Responses to Solvency argues the Affirmative points on Solvency are wrong, while Plan Attacks brings up additional reasons why the plan will not solve the harms (e.g., alternative causality the Affirmative does not take into account).

1. *Negative Philosophy.* Whereas the Affirmative offers an observation at the start of their constructive speech, the Negative offers their Negative philosophy.

This means that they establish their basic position in the round. The Negative does not simply get up and make a random series of responses to the Affirmative case, but presents a coherent line of attack. In the Negative philosophy they let the judge know what that position will be in the round.

The Negative does not just say that the Affirmative is wrong, but establishes a basic position that they will advance to win the round. For example, the Negative philosophy could be that the harms are not significant, therefore change is not necessary. Or they could argue that the problems, whether or not they are significant, can simply not be solved. Or they could argue that not only can the harms not be solved, the plan will create new problems that are worse than what we have in the *status quo*.

NOTE: The biggest concern with the Negative Constructive is that you have to cover <u>both</u> the case and the plan. In the past, most of the Negatives begin with Plan Attacks and/or Disadvantages that take up most of the time of their speech. That means they spend less time on case side, and in *some cases there are students who <u>never</u> got back to case side. That means they have granted the harms and solvency, which makes it pretty easy for the Affirmative to win the round. Why do they do this? Because the Plan Attacks and the Disadvantages are canned. But failing to cover case side is an automatic two-letter deduction on your grade, because that is not how debate rounds are supposed to go.*

The solution to this problem is simple. **Start with case side.** Make sure you have responded to the harms and solvency in the Affirmative Constructive speech before you get to the Plan Attacks and Disadvantages.

You know how long it takes you to run each Plan Attack and Disadvantage. You should literally have timing marked down on each of these attacks to know how many minutes you need to run them. If you have two Plan Attacks that are each one minute long, and a Disadvantage that is two minutes long, then you need four minutes to run plan side and that leaves you four minutes to do your Negative philosophy and case side.

Plus, the Plan Attacks can be stronger when you link them to solvency attacks.

2. *Responses to Harms.* This is where the Negative responds to the specific harms raised by the Affirmative. Keep in mind that there are three basic

ways to attack harms. First, you can argue the harms are not harms. Second, you can argue the harms are not significant. Third, you can argue the harms do not affect a significant number of people.

For example, when the class was debating free college tuition, the Affirmative would claim that because of massive student loan debt, adults were not putting off getting married, having children, and/or buying homes. The Negative could argue that putting off getting married is not a harm, because there is evidence that the younger you are when you get married, the higher the divorce rate. Waiting to get married increases the chances the marriage will last, which would be a good thing. That would be an example of the first type of result.

An example of the second would be to argue the harm is not significant because the Affirmative never argued any specific impacts. So people put off getting married. So what? How does that harm them? This can be combined with the first argument because the Negative can argue (1) that the Affirmative never argued any Negative impacts to putting off marriage (or having children), and (2) that putting off marriage and children are good things because young people can become successful in their jobs and be better able to afford those things later.

The third type of argument would be to attack the Affirmative for not quantifying how many people are supposedly harmed because they put off getting married or having children or buying a home. Are we talking ten people? A hundred? A thousand? What is the specific number? Notice that this is an argument that does not need evidence to be made. The Negative can point out the Affirmative has failed to quantify the significance of the harm.

3. *Responses to Solvency.* There are only specific planks that the Affirmative can list as their plan. While the Negative could have cards that refute the idea of being able to keep Social Security solvent, ideally you would have at least one card that was specific to each plank in the Affirmative plan.

The Affirmative is going to argue that each plan plank will either increase revenue for Social Security or decrease the amount paid out to retirees. The Negative wants to prove those things will not generate or not save the required amount of money.

The Negative can also argue that the harms will persist despite the Affirmative plan. If the harms still exist, it is hard for the Affirmative to claim they have solved them.

4. *Plan Attacks.* These are reasons why the Affirmative plan cannot solve the harms that are different from attacking the solvency of the Affirmative plan.

Usually, these have to do with alternative causality. The Affirmative has forgotten about the problems caused by X, Y and Z, all of which are reasons that they will not be able to solve the plan. For example, the Negative might argue that the Affirmative fails to account for inflation, or the recession, or the fluctuations of birth rates, death rates, and immigration that affects the number of workers. Again, I am not saying those are good lines of attack; I am just providing examples of alternative causality.

5. *Disadvantages.* There can also be general reasons why reforming Social Security is bad and also specific reasons why a given plank in the Affirmative plan will create new problems.

For example, any plan plank that reduces the amount of money paid out by Social Security is going to create problems for retirees. That would be a reason *not* to adopt the plan. Of course, the Affirmative can argue in their response to the Disadvantage that getting say 80% of your money (a number I am completely making up for the sake of this example), is better than only getting 60% of your money because Social Security is insolvent or 0% of your money if it fails (again, making up numbers, just for the purpose of this example, but you can now have a sense of how the Affirmative can respond to a Disadvantage).

Another standard type of Disadvantage is to argue that if the government spends money on Social Security, then they are diverting funds from other problems that need to be solved. The problem is that the planks of the plan have specific ways of increasing revenue, which is not the same thing as diverting funds. What would be more fruitful is arguing how losing the ability to borrow money from the Social Security Trust fund will cause problems that can only be solved by raising taxes on everybody. Then the problem is that the Disad is not unique because with or without the plan, borrowing money from Social Security is gone.

You do not want to argue a Disadvantage that the Affirmative can easily defeat, because there is the danger that they can flip it and make it an additional advantage in favor of the Affirmative.

* * * * * * *

One key thing to underscore, is that the Negative does not have to *refute* everything in the Affirmative case, but it does have to *respond* to everything. Otherwise you will be dropping points that can potentially come back to haunt you (i.e., lose you the round).

For example, if your Negative philosophy is that the harms cannot be solved, then you do not necessarily need to make counter-arguments against the harms. One of the benefits of this particular approach is that instead of running cards against any of the harms points, you can run even more cards against solvency, the voting issue that you think will be critical in winning you the round.

Similarly, you could decide the problem is not significant, and double your effort to win harms and then argue that if there is no significant problem, then solvency does not matter.

Either way, it is a strategic decision But the important thing to remember is that if, for example, the Affirmative cites three specific harms for Social Security becoming insolvent, and you only respond to one of them, then the Affirmative will point out you dropped the other two, extend them, and argue they have proven the harm is significant because you granted most of their harms.

The Negative Constructive is two minutes longer than the Affirmative Constructive, but every single negative spends more than two minutes on plan side. That means the Negative is always spending *less* time on case side than the Affirmative did. Just be sure you do not give away the two voting issues on case side because you end up spending only two minutes on harms and solvency.

Chapter 9.
Rebuttal Speeches

After the two Constructive speeches, the remaining speeches are all Rebuttals. The basic difference between a Constructive speech and a Rebuttal speech, is that you cannot bring up "new" arguments in rebuttals. So the Affirmative cannot come up with a new harm area or a new plan plank, and the Negative cannot bring up additional Plan Attacks and/or Disadvantages. You can *extend* arguments (e.g., additional things that retirees need money to pay for in order to be able to live), but you cannot bring up completely new arguments in rebuttals.

In this chapter we will cover each of the Rebuttal speeches in turn.

FIRST AFFIRMATIVE REBUTTAL

There are two things the Affirmative is doing in their First Rebuttal Speech. They are both responding to the Negative's plan side attacks and rebuilding their case by refuting the Negative's case side attacks. The Affirmative must accomplish *both* of those things, because if they only do one, then they are dropping two voting issues (harms and solvency on case side, Plan Attacks and Disadvantages on plan side).

If the Affirmative drops a voting issue, then they are probably going to lose the round (if the Negative does not notice that the Affirmative dropped a voting issue, then there is a chance the Affirmative can still win the round).

The key in this speech is having your responses worked out in advance to the plan side attacks and to have extensions available for rebuilding you're the Affirmative case.

You should have both evidence and lines of attack ready for any Plan Attacks or Disadvantages that the Negative might run against your case. In fact, because you have Plan Attacks and Disadvantages that you can run against other Affirmative cases, you can anticipate what the Negative can run against you case and make adjustments or pre-emptive arguments. After all, you know which Plan Attacks go against each of your plan planks and can anticipate those are what the Negative will run (given that they *should* run then, but be aware that sometimes the Negative runs the wrong plan attacks in a round).

So, if there are five possible Disadvantages the Negative can run against any Affirmative case, then you should have evidence and arguments to make against all five. Because you have labeled your evidence cards correctly as being NEG PA or NEG

DA, you have them ready to go. You use additional abbreviations to know which cards go with which of the cleared Plan Attacks and Disadvantages. As soon as you know what the Negative is running, you pull those cards to be able to use and put the rest away because you will not need them in this round.

Likewise, you have extension cards ready to run for each of your harms and solvency points. Not that you will always need to use them, because you will not always need to read evidence when you respond to an attack on harms or solvency. You can refer back to the evidence in your Constructive speech that the Negative failed to clash with.

For example, last year when we were debating full college tuition, Affirmatives would argue that student loan debt was leading to Americans putting off getting married, having children, and buying homes. Say the Affirmative read cards for all three points, but the Negative only read a card to respond to the first point about putting off getting married. The Affirmative would run the extension card on that harm but not the extension cards for the other two harms because the Affirmative dropped them and the evidence from the Affirmative Constructive effectively wins the point.

The Affirmative would also argue that even if they lose the getting married point, they still win the having children and buying homes points, which gives them the voting issue of Harms.

NEGATIVE REBUTTAL

The Negative's Rebuttal is their final speech in the round, so like the First Affirmative Rebuttal it is responding to the previous speech, but like the Second Affirmative Rebuttal it is also building the ballot. What voting issues does the Negative win that will win them the round?

Technically, the Negative does not need to cover everything in the round. For example, you might decide that you cannot win harms, that if Social Security fails people will indeed be significantly harmed. But your Negative Philosophy is that the Affirmative plan cannot solve the harms. In that case you briefly cover Harms, arguing that the harms would exist (but maybe would not be significant), but that the key reason to vote Negative is that the Affirmative plan cannot solve the harms. Therefore, you devote most of the time in your rebuttal speech to attacking Solvency (and showing how the Plan Attacks apply as well).

While do not need to refute everything the other side says, you do need to account for it. Saying you grant harms but that you will still win the round because you will win solvency, is enough to avoid dropping the voting issue of harms.

The last thing to do in this speech is to tell the judge and the audience why you win the round. That specifically means what voting issues you win.

Remember, the Negative does not have to win *all* of the voting issues. The Negative can win the round by winning just *one* voting issue, if it outweigh everything else.

Do not leave it to the judge to figure out how your attacks win you a voting issue. Make an explicit argument for why you win the voting issues you think you win, and explain how they win you the round. Everything you argue in a speech, whether it is a constructive speech or a rebuttal speech, should tie back to a voting issue.

SECOND AFFIRMATIVE REBUTTAL

This is the final speech of the round and it is different from the other two rebuttals. In the last speech the Affirmative is not focused on arguing out all the specific points that have been raised in the round. Instead, they are building the ballot, which means focusing more on the big picture.

What the Affirmative is doing in their 3-minute Second Rebuttal is similar to what you are doing when you write your critiques of the round.

The Affirmative boils each voting issue down to the key elements. Instead of covering all of the points that each side has raised, the Affirmative sets up what the key class is for each voting issue. Essentially, that means identifying what is the *strongest* argument for each side on that voting issue (do not make the mistake of pointing to a *weaker* argument by the Negative), and explaining why the Affirmative position is better and why they win the voting issue. You are establishing the key *clash* for each voting issue.

Note: If the Negative dropped an entire voting issue in their rebuttal, then that would be a good place to start the Second Affirmative Rebuttal, because you can quickly cover how the Negative dropped the voting issue, that your last response would have won the voting issue anyway, and that you basically have that voting issue in the bank. That becomes the first element of building the ballot.

The final point to make about the last speech in the round is that while the Affirmative is using their prep time before the speech that for each voting issue, they circle the key argument on each side. Then you do not have to write out all the arguments. For example, you circle the key evidence card from the Affirmative Constructive speech that establishes a significant harm, and then circle the key attack by the Negative in their Rebuttal speech. You can provide a brief synopsis of each argument from your flow and then argue why the Negative's card does not successfully refute your original harms evidence.

Chapter 10.
Flowing the Round

Whether you are one of the two debaters in the round or a member of the audience listening to the debate, you need to be able to flow the round. This means that you write out on sheets of paper what happens in each speech.

You would need at least two if not three pieces of paper to flow the round. The first one or two sheets would be used to flow case side, which is established in the Affirmative's Constructive speech and which will be touched upon in all five speeches in the round. The final sheet would be for plan side, which are the Plan Attacks and Disadvantages raised by the Negative in their constructive speech, which means it would be argued in just four speeches in the round (the last four).

This matters in terms of how you flow the round, because for case side your sheet of paper—which you set up **horizontally** rather than vertically—is going to have five columns (one for each speech), and your plan side sheet of paper will have four column (again, one for each speech).

The idea is to be able to trace the "flow" of the debate by having the Affirmative and Negative arguments regarding a specific point (e.g., the first harms area or the first Disadvantage), being lined up in each of the columns so that you can trace the development left to right straight across the flow.

FLOWING

A key aspect of flowing is that when you flow the Constructive speech that starts each side of the debate, that you leave enough room for the responses and the way the debate might go. Say, for the sake of argument, that the Negative decides to make three arguments against one of the harms in the 1AC. You need room to put those arguments on your flow (Also, the more space there is the easier it is to follow the flow).

HELPFUL HINT: Use some sort of symbol, such as an *, to denote when and where evidence is used in the round because you can see immediately on your flow whether or not a claim is supported with evidence. Abbreviations will also come in handy when flowing: "SS" for Social Security, "CONG" for Congress, "JB" for Joe Biden, "→" for causes, etc.

Keep in mind that the goal is to be able to chart the "flow" of an argument over the course of the debate. You should be able to literally see if on your flow sheets (you received a sample of a debate flow on the first day of class along with this handbook).

111 | P a g e

When you flow the initial speeches on case side and plan side, space out the initial arguments, because when the Affirmative presents three harms areas in their constructive speech, the Negative might respond with 2 or 3 points for *each* of those three harms areas. So as you flow the three harms you leave space between them to be able to accommodate how the Negative responds to each.

If you did not do this, your flow might look like this:

A. First Harm   →   1. First response to the
                                  First Harm
B. Second Harm   2. Second response
C. Third Harm   3. Third response

Where would you flow the responses to the Second and Third Harms? They would be further down on the page (opposite Solvency?). Instead you want it to look like this:

A. First Harm →   1. First response to the First
Harm
                     2. Second response
                     3. Third response

B. Second Harm → 1. First response to the Second
                        Harm
                    2. Second response

C. Third Harm →   1. First response to the Third
                        Harm
                    2. Second response

Again, the goal is to have all of the responses line up across the flow:

Aff Harm → Neg Const. → Aff Rebuttal → Neg Rebuttal → Aff Reb.

SIGNPOSTING

It is important that everybody—the debaters, the judge, and the audience—know where we are on the flow of the debate. For that reason, signposting arguments is key. If you are arguing a point about Harms 1 or Solvency B, you need to signpost accordingly. Main points need to be signposted as the A point, B point, etc.

When you have more than one response to an argument, then you should number them so you can refer back to them later in the round (if you have more than one piece of evidence for an argument, then you should definitely have separate signposted points you are making).

One advantage of numbering your responses is that you make it clear to the judge that you have multiple points of attack. It is not just one giant point, but two or three specific attacks (and if your opponent does not respond specifically to all of them, then you can argue they were dropped and explain why they are significant in winning the round).

For example, if in your speech you refer to "My opponents second response on the B point of my Harms Contention," that should lead everybody to the same point on the Flow of the round.

Always make it perfectly clear where your arguments and evidence are to be written on the flow. Signposting makes this a piece of cake, but only if you clearly signpost your arguments and use that signposting throughout the debate.

* * * * * * *

Early in the semester one class period will be devoted to a "practice" round in which I will do all five speeches (not the cross-examinations), using totally made-up evidence. The purpose will be to allow you to practice flowing a round.

Always make sure you space out the original case side arguments of the Affirmative and the plan side arguments of the Negative. You know how Affirmative cases are structured, so you know to leave room for harms and solvency (or, better yet, use different sheets for harms and solvency). There will be an observation and two or three harms points, so basically each gets one-fourth of the sheet of paper, right? Then there will be the plan planks and two or three solvency points, so space out things accordingly.

One thing that a lot of debaters do when flowing a debate is to use two different color pens, one for each side. Either they always flow the Affirmative in blue and the Negative in black, or they are always black and their opponent is always blue.

Chapter 11.
How to Lose a Round

It will sound strange, but before you learn how to win a debate, you really have to learn how *not* to lose. When you are dealing with novice debaters, the team that "wins" is usually the team that "loses" the least in the round.

Therefore, this chapter is devoted to covering the six key ways in which novice debaters lose a round, so that can avoid doing so in your debates.

THE FIRST WAY: DROPS

The number one was to lose the round is to "drop" something.

Dropping something means that you did not offer a response to something your opponent argued. In your initial practice rounds, you are going to drop things. Your opponent is going to drop things.

For example, your opponent is the Affirmative and in their Constructive Speech they say there are two problems with the current system when we debated having free tuition for public colleges. First, there say that the cost of college is so high that it is prohibitive. Second, they say that student loan debt means college graduates are putting off major life milestones.

So there is one problem that exists before you get into college and there is another that exists once you leave college (there are also problems with students dropping out or having grades decline because they have to work to live, not just to pay for college).

Now, you would have Negative evidence for both of these contentions, because you will not be allowed to debate in class if you have not been cleared to do so, and the only way you get cleared is if you prove you have enough cards to run for and against each topic area. Otherwise you have nothing to argue in a round, which hurts the grade of your opponent who needs to respond to your arguments.

But the Negative begins their constructive by running two Plan Attacks and two Disadvantages, so when they get to case side, they read a card against the first harm, but not the second. That means they drop the second harm area, which means the Affirmative can say they win that particular point and that voting issue. Hopefully the Negative got to the Affirmative's solvency points, otherwise they will have dropped those as well.

If you do not make an argument, then how does your opponent respond?

Let's take the second contention first. The Affirmative argues that massive student load debt means college graduates are putting off (a) getting married and (b) buying a house. Your response is to read a blurb card that says students are <u>not</u> putting off getting married. This is a problem for two reasons. First, it so happens the Affirmative's (A) card cites the percentage of college graduates who report they are doing exactly that, which means you have failed to clash with their specific arguments. Second, you did not talk about putting off buying a house, which means you dropped the (B) card.

It is hard to take out two separate points with one card. It can be done, but those are usually not easy cards to find.

Meanwhile, on the first contention, the Negative reads a card, so the Affirmative needs to show how the Negative's evidence does not refute the original Affirmative point, and perhaps read an extension card on that first harm. After all, the Negative dropped the second harm so you do not need to read a card there. Running an extension card on what they *did* respond to would be a good move.

THE SECOND WAY: NOT HAVING A *PRIMA FACIE* CASE

Prima facie is a Latin phrase that means the Affirmative has the responsibility, as part of the

Burden of Proof, to put everything they need in their constructive speech to win the debate

They cannot, for example, run nothing but harms cards in their Constructive speech and then run the solvency cards in the First Affirmative Rebuttal.

To be fair, nobody has tried to do that. But what has happened is that instead of having two contentions, some debaters try to get in THREE, and since they only have six minutes, they run out of time and never get to Solvency on Contention III.

The first questions the Negative will ask in the Cross-X period is "Did you read any Solvency evidence on Contention 3?" The Affirmative will admit they did not. At the start of Case Side in the Negative Constructive the Negative will say there was no evidence for solvency on Contention 3, so that Contention is gone. The Affirmative cannot bring up a completely new Solvency argument in their First Rebuttal Speech.

The Affirmative has to provide evidence for both Harms (including Significance) and Solvency in their Constructive speech, otherwise they have not established a prima facie case.

This should not be a problem because not only do you have to clear all the evidence you are using in your Affirmative Constructive, you will submit an outline with the specific cards you will be using. If your cards do not prove significance or do not prove solvency, I am going to tell you that and insist you find cards that do, so you have a prima facie case.

THE THIRD WAY: NOT TO HAVE EVIDENCE.

This most often happens on Solvency with the Affirmative. They find all these great harms, but did not find a card that argues the Affirmative plan will solve that harm. So they will just say the plan solves the harms rather than present actual evidence.

Sometimes this is not a problem, because if, for example, the harm is the government in drafting young men and sending them off to fight in a foreign war (Harm) and the plan is the end the draft, then that pretty much solves the problem.

But if you are arguing that providing free public college tuition will solve the problem of putting off life milestones, you need a card that argues exactly that (e.g., there are other countries that have had success in forgiving student loan debt. Yes, a foreign country is not the U.S.A., but that card is way better than nothing or a blurb asserting solvency).

Again, all of the initial assignments in this class are devoted to finding you the evidence you need for both Affirmative and Negative on each of the specific things you will be arguing in rounds.

THE FOURTH WAY: HAVE BAD EVIDENCE.

Now, going in to this section let me once again say that you should not have bad evidence because every time you submit evidence, I will tell you which cards and cleared and which are not. I will provide a specific reason that the card is no good, or tell you specifically how it needs to be improved (I had one student who submitted Affirmative cards as Negative evidence: if they had run those in a round the Affirmative would say "Thank you very much for providing additional evidence to prove my case").

One of the reasons you need to find at least three cards for each topic in terms of both harms and solvency, is so that you can find the BEST evidence and not just the easiest evidence to find for each point.

Actually, the biggest problem with "bad evidence" is that the Affirmative runs Harms areas X and Z, and the Negative reads evidence for Harms area Y instead. That is "bad evidence" because it does not clash with the Affirmative points. They argue Apples and Oranges and the Negative argues Zebras. The Negative has not "dropped" the Affirmative's point, but they failed to offer a legitimate response and all the Affirmative has to do is point that out to win the point (and the voting issue).

For that matter, even if the Affirmative does *not* point that out, the Judge can still give the Affirmative the point because evidence was just plain bad.

THE FIFTH WAY: HAVE AN ATTACK TURNED

Sometimes the Affirmative can turn—or "flip"—a Negative argument and make it a reason to vote Affirmative.

For example, last year when we were debating free public college tuition, there were five possible harms topics the Affirmative could run:

1. High tuition makes it difficult for people to go to college.
2. Financial concerns affect grades and graduation.
3. Student Loans/Financial Aid to not provide enough assistance.
4. Student debt delays major milestones for people.
5. Student debt causes health problems.

Now, the Negative is supposed to have five Plan Attacks ready, one for each Affirmative topic. In this particular round the two Affirmative Harms are (4) and (5). What happens after graduation.

But instead of running the specific Plan Attacks they have against those two harms; the Negative runs their Plan Attacks against (1) and (2).

The Affirmative, overjoyed at the opportunity, has two responses for each of those Plan Attacks.

1. I did not claim to solve for those problems in my Affirmative case, so the Negative is granting solvency. But at the very least, they are not clashing with my contentions.

2. I am going to Turn/Flip each of those Plan Attacks because even though I am not running those two contention, I only got cleared to debate in the round because I have harms and solvency evidence for ALL of them. Which means I can run one of my solvency cards for each Plan Attack and claim I flip the Plan Attacks into ADDITIONAL CONTENTIONS supporting the Affirmative case.

They make the same argument for both Plan Attacks, and contend they now have FOUR contentions in support of the Resolution.

THE SIXTH WAY: RUN ARGUMENTS THAT ARE NOT CLEARED

What if the Affirmative runs a harm or a Plan Attack or something that is not cleared? You are not going to have any evidence for something that is not one of the five approved topics. This is not fair.

Of course, it is not. All you do is point out in your constructive speech that the Affirmative did not present a Prima Facie case, because they did not prove significant harms and solvency for one of the give topic areas.

The same thing applies to the Negative if they were to run a Plan Attack or a Disadvantage that had not been cleared. Again, there are limits on what can be argued for Plan Attacks and Disadvantages, just as there are for harms and solvency. You point out that the attack is not from the list of cleared ones, and move on to other parts of the debate where there are key clashes to resolve.

Okay, but what if the Negative says nothing, or only speaks two minutes instead of eight, or drops both solvency points or some combination of all that?

That is what we will be covering in the next chapter: how to deal with drops.

Chapter 12.
Dealing with Dropped Points

What do you do if your opponent says nothing in their speech?

Okay, your opponent is not going to say *nothing* in their speech because if they showed up for the round, then they are going to have to say something. At the very least they have all those evidence cards that they can read.

But what if….

- They spend all of their time on Plan Attacks and/or Disadvantages and never get back to case side?
- They talk about harms but not solvency?
- They talk about the first harms card but not the second harms card?
- Or any combination of those things.

Things always get dropped in a round. Always. There are so many things to talk about not everything will get covered, so things will *always* get dropped.

What if the Negative never responds to one or more of your contentions?

1. You point out that the contention was dropped.

2. You argue that you win the specific voting issue that was dropped: harms, significance, and solvency.

3. That wins you the contention, but there is also the time concern, because you were planning on taking a minute or more to rebuild your contention. You do not want to repeat everything you said in your constructive speech. But what you can do is read an extension card.

Example A: In your Affirmative Constructive you cite a study that proves X. In your First Affirmative Rebuttal, you can run a card that offers a second study that further proves the point, or perhaps a card that says the consensus of studies proves X. Of course, this is a card you can run against the Negative if they *do* say something, to refute their attack and extend your point and hammer home that you win the voting issue.

Example B: When the topic was Free College Tuition, one of the harms areas was that student debt delayed adult milestones. If you run a first harms card that said people were delaying getting married and having children, and a second harms card that talks about delaying home ownership, an extension card for the rebuttal would be about delaying saving for retirement. It extends the argument by expanding the harms area (all stemming from the same cause, so it is not a *new* argument in rebuttals).

The same approach works if the Affirmative drops a Negative Plan Attack or Disadvantage.
But what if the Negative says absolutely *nothing* in the round? They showed up—otherwise the round in class would be cancelled and it would be made up on ZOOM at a later time—but they hem and haw for a minute and then sit down.

At which point you have to cross-examine them and basically cover how they dropped everything, which would be a different type of headache. But, just for the sake of argument, what if the Negative never made any attacks or read any evidence?

In this worst-case scenario—which should not happen because the Negative has been cleared to debate which means they have cards for Harms and Solvency for all five topic areas, plus Plan Attacks or Disadvantages for both—you would simply run all of the arguments and extension cards you have prepared for when your points *are* attacked.

At the very least you go over your points, and build your ballot. You established a harm. You established that it was significant. There was no response by the Negative so both of those are granted. But you also argue that you evidence was solid to begin with (so it is more YOU win, than THEY lose). So you have that voting issue.

You can also present extension evidence. For each harm, solvency, Plan Attack or Disadvantage you should have at least three cards (each making a different point). While you use the best card(s) for your constructive, you can run the other cards as extensions.

Because there are a limited number of Plan Attacks and Disadvantages that the Negative can run against the Affirmative, you would be prepared to respond to anything and everything that might be argued. So, in theory, you could do a competent First Affirmative Rebuttal even before you hear the Negative attacks because you have arguments and evidence prepared. You just need to know what plan side attacks the Negative is actually using in the round.

What you do not want to do is to avoid using all of your speaking time, because there are point deductions for being under the time limit. If you were a minute short, then that would be at least a grade deduction. This is because with all of the preparation you did putting your evidence together you really have *too much* to say in any given speech.

You should never be significantly under-time with any of your speeches.

Chapter 13.
Cross-Examination

After each of the constructive speeches by the Affirmative and Negative speakers, they are cross-examined (known as Cross-X) by their opponent for three-minutes. Reminder: this happens immediately after the speech is over and before the speaker asking questions uses their two minutes of prep-time.

TYPES OF CROSS-X QUESTIONS

There are three categories of questions that you can ask your opponent.

First, you can ask questions of clarification. This covers relatively minor things like getting the signposting and the claims made by the points right.

- What was the date on the second harms card?
- What are the credentials of your source on the Solvency B point?
- Did you read a card for Solvency A?

Second, you can ask questions to expose holes in your opponent's case. This would begin with something like a drop. If the Negative did not 8 respond to all of the specific points raised by the Affirmative—for example, touching only on only one of the three specific types of harms—then the Affirmative would want to point out the drop, and then they would want to be sure to argue that in their next speech.

- How much additional revenue will your first plan plank provide?
- How much does the average retiree need each month to survive?
- If you cut Social Security benefits, then what will retirees be forced to give up to be able to survive?
- How does your plan account for Cost-of-Living Adjustments?

You do not want to expose things in your opponent's constructive that you do not follow up on. Getting them to admit that they did not provides the qualifications for several of their sources does not matter if you are not going to argue that your sources are better in your next speech.

Third, you can ask questions that set up the arguments you are going to make in your next speech. This usually has to do with setting up Plan Attacks and Disadvantages by getting the Affirmative to admit to the link needed to have them apply.

- If you increase the tax rate to pay for Social Security, how will that adversely affect the economy?
- How many new workers will the Social Security Administration need to be able to make this plan work?

Understand that nothing that is said in the cross-examination impacts the round. If, for example, the Affirmative admits they do not have solvency for one of their harms, that does not matter unless the Negative makes an argument in their constructive speech that the Affirmative does not have solvency. The cross-examination is not flowed, so it is not part of the round in terms of determining who wins specific points and voting issues.

P.S. One thing you will notice by the time we are halfway through the debates this semester, is that in Cross-X you can clearly see how much everybody in this class knows about the topic. Also, that Cross-X is probably more like how you will "debate" in the real world than anything else you do in this class.

WHAT TO AVOID IN ASKING CROSS-X QUESTIONS

Avoid making a statement rather than asking a question. The cross-examination period is not when you get to make an argument. It is for asking questions. If you do not follow the *Jeopardy* rule and put it in the form of a question, then do not be surprised when your opponent points out it was not a question.

Because if it was not a question, then they do not need to answer it, right?

Conversely, the person being questioned does not get to ask questions. This is not their Cross-X.

Again, since your opponent cannot ask questions, then you do not need to answer it.

However, there are situations where the respondent might ask a question of clarification: e.g., Are you asking about the second Plan Attack? Which card are you asking about? Those are fine, because they facilitate getting the right information.

Avoid asking really long-winded questions. It should take around 10 seconds to ask a question. You do not want to be taking half a minute to ask a question.

Similarly, avoiding giving really long answers. Yes, that takes away the cross-examination from the person asking the questions, but that is not the goal. Also, the person who is asking the question has the right to cut off long-winded answers.

Ideally, you should be able to have three questions asked and answered in a minute, which means you should get to at least nine exchanges in the three-minute period.

PREPARING FOR CROSS-X

You can prepare lists of possible cross-X questions that you can ask in a round. After all, at the very least, you know what you can argue on each side with regards to each topic area. Your Affirmative case will be put together being aware of what the Negative can run against you because you have researched both sides and have evidence for each side.

This is another place where you can use index cards. For each specific harm, plan plank, plan attack and disadvantage you can have a separate card with list of questions specific to that particular topic. If your potential questions are not arranged most to least important, then you can make use some sort of symbol (e.g., a star) to indicate what question or questions it would be most important for you to ask.

NOTE: You do not want to just have a list of 20 questions because how would you know which ones to run in a round? Organize them by harm areas and by Plan Attacks and Disadvantages. Then, based on what your opponent is running, you can *find the possible questions you can ask specific to those points.*

Some questions will not be on your list because they will be determined by what you discover flowing your opponent's constructive speech. Did they not offer evidence on a specific point? Are the credentials of one of their sources suspect (e.g., they are just a politician and not an expert in the field).

Also, do not forget about the value of asking follow up questions on key issues. A follow up question can help your opponent dig a bigger hole for themselves in the round.

Chapter 14.
Critiquing a Round

Once we start going graded debates you will either be one of the two debaters or you will be critiquing the debate.

Unlike the public speaking class you took, critiquing your classmates is not simply an academic exercise. Granted, there is value in not only delivering speeches in public speaking but in also critiquing them, because you can learn from others. But here you are, one or more semesters after having taken public speaking, and while you hopefully remember what you did for all of your speeches in that class, how many of the speeches given by *other* students do you actually remember? There are probably a few, that stick out in your mind for one reason or another, but nobody is going to remember most of the speeches they heard.

In debate class there is a significant difference because in addition to rendering a judgment on who won each voting issue and who won the round overall, you can find arguments and evidence in those rounds that you can use in your own debates.

NOTE: Your critique of the round that you submit to be graded is essentially the same as the Second

Affirmative Rebuttal: it does not go through all the points made in all of the speeches with regards to a particular voting issue. Instead, it takes each voting issue, establishes what you thought was the best argument/evidence on each side, and then argues out who wins the voting issue and why. Of course, in each round the Affirmative is going to say they *win each voting issue, but in your critique you make a judgment for each voting issues as to who wins.*

The last paragraph in your critique explains who wins the round *based on the decisions you already made on who wins each voting issue* in the previous paragraphs.

If one side wins all of the voting issues, then obviously they win the round. If one side wins *most* of the voting issues, then they will probably win the round, but it depends. Let us say, for the sake of argument, that the Affirmative wins both harms and solvency: their plan will solve their harms. The Negative's Plan Attacks did not take away from solvency, so the Affirmative wins them as well. But what if the Negative had a Disadvantage that proves the Affirmative plan will cause global thermonuclear war and destroy all life on Earth. Well, in that case the one voting issue of that Disadvantage would outweigh the Affirmative solving the harms.

Yes, that is an extreme example, but remember that if the Negative can win *one* voting issue, they can argue that is enough to win them the round. If there is no significant harm, then there is no reason to vote Affirmative. If the Affirmative cannot solve their harms, then that is a good reason not to vote Affirmative. If the Affirmative causes more significant problems as established in a Disad, then that is another good reason not to vote Affirmative.

SAMPLE CRITIQUE

Here is a sample critique from several semesters back when each side had to argue the value by which they thought should be the basis for judging the Affirmative plan (we do not do that anymore). Also, that year the Negative was not running separate Plan Attacks, just attacking solvency.

The topic had to do with "defunding the police," which actually had to do with reallocating money to other services or pulling funding from military weapons and not actually stop funding the police.

The key thing here is that you can see how for each voting issue the critique establishes the strongest argument on each side and then explains why they think the Affirmative won. Even though the Affirmative won all of the voting issues, notice that the last paragraph does not just state that is the case and stop there, but actually explains how those voting issues add up to the round.

* * * * * * *

The Affirmative value was equality and the best argument was that when cases are treated as others with situations being the same and there are equal resources to aid minorities. The Negative value was safety and the best argument was when citizens are protected from threats and the police department is supported so they can do their job. I believe the Affirmative won because safety doesn't overpower equality and the criteria for equality were very strong.

I think the best argument on harms for the Affirmative was Black people are at more of risk, 2.5% more. The Negatives best argument was that police recruitment and numbers will drop resulting in issues. I believe the Affirmative won, overall their first contention was really strong with the statistics and comparing the numbers by race and gender.

The Affirmative best argument for solvency was that police shouldn't have the right to social programs, they have a lot going on and it could be done better by an outreached source. The Negative's best argument was that if numbers are dropping, we can't be picky with who we chose to be an officer and that will result in more bad cops. I believe the Affirmative won because it showed that the harms can be solved and I also think the Negative highlighted that there are bad cops in the system.

The Affirmative best argument for the Disadvantage is that minorities overall aren't being treated

equally and we could be doing better. The Negatives best argument for a Disadvantage was that the community won't be protected if we defund the police and the public will be at risk or crime. I believe that the Affirmative won because it showed a big
Disadvantage that seemed to outweigh the Negatives.

Overall I think that the Affirmative won all the voting issues, she started out strong winning her value because equality overpowers safety. She won her harms and solvency because they worked well together, and gave evidence that the minorities in the community were already at harm and feeling unsafe. The Disadvantage was clear and
showed real issues that can arise and already have been present.

Overall I believe the Affirmative won all the voting issues and it was really solid.

* * * * * * *

Again, keep in mind that what you do in a critique is similar to what the Affirmative should be doing in their Second Rebuttal: Arguing what is the key clash on each voting issue, what the best arguments are on *both* sides, and then arguing why one side (your side) wins the voting issues and therefore the round.

Also, I should mention that whether you win or lose the round does not impact your grades on the speeches and cross-examinations in each round. Usually whoever "wins" the round ends up with the higher score, but not always, because the Affirmative could do a great job on arguing everything but drop a Disad that the Negative successfully argues outweighs the Affirmative case. The Affirmative would end up with higher grades on everything, but still technically lose the round.

The key thing is that you debate well. That you clash with the other side's arguments, that you have solid evidence, that you signpost where everything goes, and you argue out the warrants and voting issues. Doing those things are what determines your grades.

ABBREVIATIONS AND ACRONYMS

AC: Alternative causality

AFF: Affirmative

CA: Comparative advantage

COLA: Cost of living adjustment

CON: Constructive

CONG: Congress

CPI: Consumer Price Index

CX: Cross examination

DA: Disadvantage

FRA: Full retirement age

H: Harm

IRS: Internal Revenue Service

JB: President Joe Biden

NEG: Negative

NP: Negative philosophy

OBS: Observation

OASDI: Old-Age, Survivors, and Disability Insurance program

PA: Plan Attack

REB: Rebuttal

SIG: Significance

SOLV: Solvency

SS: Social Security

SSA: Social Security Administration

VI: Voting issue

W: Warrant

VOCABULARY TERMS

Affirmative: Argues in favor of the resolution. The Affirmative side is responsible for introducing the resolution, listing the claims that support their argument along with evidence and reasoning, and refuting the Negatives' arguments.

Alternative Causality: A Negative argument that the harms are caused by things other than what the Affirmative claims, which leads to reduced solvency because they cannot completely solve the problem.

Argument: A complete argument consists of a claim, evidence, and a warrant explaining how the evidence supports the claim.

Argumentation: Using evidence and reasoning to support claims.

Block: A block is when one side, usually the Negative, has several points and/or cards to make against the Affirmative. Instead of having all of the evidence on separate cards, you have all of the arguments and evidence on a sheet of paper, because you are making all of those points in your speech.

Burden of Proof: Because the Negative (*status quo*) has *presumption*, the Affirmative has the burden of proof to come up with reasons and evidence to change the current system. This is why the Affirmative gets both the first and last speeches in the round. Because they have to meet the burden of proof to win the debate.

Card: A piece of evidence, usually a quote from an expert that proves a point.

Claim: Controversial statement that a debater supports or refutes with evidence and reasoning. To be a claim, a statement must have at least two sides so that it is in dispute. "Schools should run year-round" is a claim; "Wednesday comes after Tuesday" is not (it is an indisputable fact).

Comparative Advantage: Argument that the Affirmative solves the harm better than the *status quo*, and therefore has a comparative advantage over the *status quo*. The Affirmative argument is that it does not solve *all* of the harms, but that it solves significantly *more* than the *status quo*.

Constructive Speech: A speech that presents a debater's basic arguments for or against the resolution.

Contention: A large argument or set of smaller arguments that support a case. They often have sub-points.

Cross Examination: The period during a debate when a member of one team asks questions of an opposing team member to obtain additional information about their arguments and positions.

Debate: The process of arguing the Affirmative or Negative side of a resolution against an opposing team, often including a judge or audience or who decides the outcome.

Disadvantage: A Negative argument that the Affirmative plan will create a new harm that does not currently exist. The Disadvantage has to be non-topical: If the Affirmative plan provides for free college tuition, then the Disadvantage would be that the government would have to cut money from other vital services to pay for it.

Drop: When a debater does not address or respond to a subpoint or argument. In other words, they did not refute it, so they implicitly agree with it. However, drops must be impacted to count. It is not enough to say your opponent did not refute your argument, you must say why it matters (impacting--why that point is important, and the fact that your opponent agrees with you means you win the round).

Evidence: Information used to support a claim. All of your evidence in these debates will be on index cards (or sheets of paper for blocks).

Extend: To carry across the flow. Debaters literally draw an arrow from one speech to the next to indicate that the same point is being argued in both speeches.

Fallacy, or Logical Fallacy: Bad or erroneous reasoning that results in an unsound argument.

Fiat: Latin for "let it be done." A theoretical construct in policy debate whereby the substance of the resolution is debated, rather than the political feasibility of enactment and enforcement of a given plan, allowing an Affirmative team to "imagine" a plan into being.

Flip: When one side takes an argument against them and turns it into an argument *for* them. Usually done to Disadvantages or Plan Attacks. The Negative argues the Affirmative plan will increase X, which is something other than the topic; the Affirmative proves that the Affirmative plan actually decreases X, and therefore turns the Disadvantage into an advantage, flipping the Disad.

Flowing: Taking notes during a debate in order to keep a record of what's been said and prepare for refutations and cross examinations.

Granting: If your opponent fails to respond to a specific argue (i.e., "drops" it), then you can argue that they have granted you the point, which you can then use to build your argument for winning that particular voting issue.

Grouping: Usually used in the context of "Group these sub-points together." It is just what it sounds like: the debater is addressing several points at once by responding to the underlying idea behind them. This is more common in the latter speeches where there is less time to cover everything.

Harm: Something bad that happens because of the position one side takes.

Impact: Explains the *importance* of the warranted claim. For harms this is showing that what is happening to people is both bad and significant. The same thing would apply for the Disadvantages.

Judges: Individuals who listen to debate, decide the winner, rank debate competitors, and ensure that the experience is educational for all participants in a debate competition.

Negative: Argues against the resolution and the Affirmative team's arguments for significant change. The Negative states the claims that support their position, provides evidence and reasoning, and refutes the Affirmatives' arguments.

Plan: The Affirmative proposal for changing the *status quo*.

Plan Attack: An argument raised by the Negative that argues why the plan will not work. This is an attack on Solvency. The difference is a response of Solvency says "the Affirmative says X will work, but it will not," while a Plan Attack argues "X will not work because there are other factors the Affirmative is not taking into account."

Planks: The individual elements of the plan. If the Affirmative increases taxes and also reduces benefits, each of those would be a unique plank in the Affirmative plan.

Presumption: The *status quo* (current system) enjoys presumption. We presume that the current system is the best possible one, which is why the Affirmative has the burden of proof for convincing the judge there should be a change.

Reasoning: Using analysis to connect the evidence to the claim. An argument using reasoning might look like this:

- "All humans should be vegetarians (claim)
- "because animal farming is one of the primary causes of deforestation, which reduces oxygen in our atmosphere (evidence).
- "This means that farming is destroying our planet by causing severe climate change just so we can raise animals to be slaughtered for food (reasoning).
- "Therefore, all human beings should be vegetarians" (conclusion).

Rebuttal Speeches: Speeches in debate that challenge and defend arguments introduced in constructive speeches. In policy debate, each of the two debaters on each side does one constructive and one rebuttal speech. In our format each debater does one constructive and then the Affirmative does two rebuttals and the Negative one.

Refutation: The process of attacking an opponent's arguments. An organized attack on opponents' arguments. Refutation is not simply arguing the opposite side of the opposing team. It is the practice of specifically addressing the evidence or reasoning of an opponent, exposing weaknesses and undermining arguments.

Resolution: The topic or claim being debated. The resolution is always presented as an affirmative statement by the Affirmative, who has the burden of proving the truth of the resolution. To clarify the resolution being argued, it begins with the word "resolved."

Signpost: To indicate where you are on the flow. For example: "In my opponent's second contention subpoint A, they said [tagline]..." Second contention subpoint A can be abbreviated C2A.

Solvency: A contention that argues the Affirmative plan solves for the harms they have established.

Status Quo: The current system, which enjoys presumption. Specifically, the way the current system deals with the topic area.

Tagline: The one-sentence summary of a contention of subpoint. For example: Community standards have a "chilling effect" on teachers which is detrimental to the education of high school students. Or, "the chilling effect."

Voting Issue: There are four possible voting issues. Harms, Solvency, Plan Attacks, and Disadvantages. The first two are only raised by the Affirmative and the other two are only raised by the Negative.

Warrant: A reason why an assertion is true; it links the evidence to the claim. If the claim is "Cheese is good," a possible warrant would be "Cheese has nutrients."

BIBLIOGRAPHY

America Counts Staff, "2020 Census Will Help Policymakers Prepare for the Incoming Wave of Aging Boomers," *census.gov,* December 10, 2019.

Anspach, Dana, "How to Know When to Take Social Security," *thebalancemoney.com*, October 5, 2021.

Congressional Budget Office, "CBO's 2023 Long-Term Projections for Social Security," *cbo.gov,* June 29, 2023.

Congressional Budget Office, "CBO's Long-Term Social Security Projections: Changes Since 2018 and Comparisons With the Social Security Trustees' Projections," *cbo.gov,* December 12, 2019.

Congressional Budget Office, "How Changing Social Security Could Affect Beneficiaries and the System's Finances," *cbo.gov,* Accessed July 5, 2023.

Gaille, Louise. "14 Chief Pros and Cons of Social Security," *Vittana.org,* August 16, 2018.

Margenau, Tom. *Social Security: 100 Myths and 100 Facts: Setting the Record Straight About America's Most Popular and Most Misunderstood Government Program.* Creators Publishing: September 9, 2022.

Markowitz, Andy. "10 Social Security Myths That Refuse to Die," *AARP*, August 25, 2020 (Updated April 11, 2023).

Romig, Kathleen, "What the 2020 Trustees' Report Shows About Social Security," *cbpp.org*, May 13, 2020.

Social Security Administration, Briefing Paper No. 2020-01, "Analysis of Benefit Estimates Shown in the *Social Security Statement*," *ssa.gov,* October 2020.

Social Security Administration, "Frequently Asked Questions: Ratio of Covered Workers to Beneficiaries," *ssa.gov* (accessed August 17, 2015).

Vernon, Steve. "Does Congress Raid Social Security?," *cbsnews.com*, October 11, 2012.

CLEARED TOPICS

HARMS

1.

2.

3.

4.

5.

PLAN PLANKS / SOLVENCY

1.

2.

3.

4.

5.

PLAN ATTACKS

1.

2.

3.

4.

5.

DISADVANTAGES

1.

2.

3.

4.

5.

Made in the USA
Monee, IL
02 August 2023

40347626R00087